BAD   WORDS   DICTIONARY ™
and
even   worse   expressions

by
Voy   Sobon

dedicated
to
my wife
Michiho

Published by Bona Fide, Inc., New York, NY

ISBN 0-9651398-0-8
ISBN 0-9651398-1-6

9 8 7 6 5 4 3 2 1

SHIT! I HATE IT WHEN PEOPLE CURSE ME IN FOREIGN LANGUAGES AND I CAN'T RETURN THE COMPLIMENT ...

Have curses left You speechless? Have You been frustrated by the vernacular? Have You been in a neighborhood where it sort of sounded like English, but You didn't understand a word? Sometimes the intonation of the speaker gives a clue, but if "asshole" sounds hostile all over the world, why should You be left without an appropriate response, even if the insult is in **Spanish, German, French, Dutch or Japanese?**

If You're choking, there's always the Heimlich Maneuver. But when anger is in Your craw, it's harder to get rid of. Insulted and speechless... red-faced...body-twisted, You merely become an object of ridicule, provoking laughter in Your torment.

Now You can eliminate this type of embarrassing situation. **The Bad Words Dictionary** ™ gives You the ammunition to fight back in six languages, with more to come.

The staunch, straightlaced proponents of **"dull"** morality deny the existence of vulgarity.

But they are **WRONG**. Since man first learnd to communicate, obscenities have occupied a proud and useful position in our daily vocabulary. For the connoisseur of language, the lack of idiom should never stand between emotion and expression. Those of us who value culture must work to preserve this scorned, yet rich tradition. Like the hard working roach, vulgarity is hard to kill .

If poetry is the soul of a culture, then vulgarity is its body. And like the body, it grows and grows. Every social group has its own slang, which differs from generation to generation and even from block to block.

For this reason, we are conscious of our linguistic limitations. We hope, dear Reader, that You will offer Your advice and opinions so that together, we can work to improve future editions of this indispensable dictionary.

Please, write to :

Bona Fide, Inc.
331 West 57th Street, Suite 186
New York , NY 10019

DIRECTIONS FOR USE

Like the chore faced by France's truffle hunting pigs, assemling a multiplicity of drastic expressions into one fragrant basket was no easy task. We sometimes had to cross invisible borders of obscenity. In some cases, finding literal translations was impossible because im-precations and indignities are not a matter of systematic order, but an emotional catharsis.

WARNING: Many expressions and words which appear in this book should be used with the greates discretion and at Your own risk . The author can not be responsible for any reactions and physical retaliation these words may provoke.

This uncommon dictionary is assembled in alphabetical order in the English language . The guy from the cover, **Pete the pig**®, will show You the way .

In some cases, You may need to use a pocket dictionary to find common usage for certain everyday words in a particular language.

Please feel free to compose Your own.

CREDITS:

The author would like to express his heart-felt appreciation to the many esteemed scholars who labored to assist him in the creation of this important work of art.

The author regrets, however, that he can not name these masters of perverse dialects - at their own request - for fear of destroying their academic careers .

Mr. Sobon also regrets that he cannot thank the world' s major religious organizations. He had fully intended to do so, but through some inexplicable oversight, **none** of them has yet recognized the **Bad Words Dictionary' s** ™ major contribution to the advancement of world culture.

ABOUT THE AUTHOR ...

Voy Sobon was born sometime ago somewhere in the last car of a runaway train bound to Nowhere. Moments after his birth, his parents, horrified by his repulsive appearance, resolved to leave him in a remote desert, expecting that he would provide a nutritious dinner for friendly, wild animals. But even these starving beasts refused to accept him.

One sunny day, he was picked up by beautiful, free-spirited Gypsies, who raised him to be an independent man.

Mr. Voy Sobon graduated many never-opened Universities and won several never-given honors in the Strange Arts. Presently, he is happily traveling the world collecting the very best curses for the next volumes of his **Bad Words Dictionary** ™

Voy laments that although he speaks so many languages, no one seems to understand his good intentions.

Maybe some time, dear Reader, you will be shocked to encounter **Voy**, no doubt in a bizarre situation or a disgusting enviroment .

But then, please, do not judge him harshly, for he is very, very, very sensitive .

A

is for...

Asshole

English	Spanish	German
AC/DC *[ay-see dee-see]* Bisexual. Goes either way.	**Doble corriente** *[doh-blay koh-rree-ehn-tay]*	**Gleichstrom** *[glysh-struhm]*
Acid head *[ah- sid hed]* Someone who does L.S.D.	**Drogata** *[droh-gah-tah]*	**Fixer** *[fix-ah]*
Act up *[akt ahp]* Cause trouble.	**Busca pleitos** *[boo-skah play-tohss]*	**Sich aufspielen** *[zish auf-spee-len]*
Air head *[ayr hed]* Someone whoís out of it. Spaced out.	**Cabeza de serrín** *[kah-beh-thah deh seh-rreen]*	**Hirngespinst** *[hearn-guh-shpinst]*
Alky *[ahl-kee]* Someone who is an alcoholic.	**Borracho** *[boh-rrah-choh]*	**Alki** *[ahl-kee]*
Ambulance chaser *[ahm-byoo-lahnss chay-ssehr]* A personal injury lawyer with minimal ethics.	**Leguleyo** *[leh-goo-lay-yoh]*	**Ambulanzjäger** *[am-byu-lans-yay-gah]*

French	Dutch	Japanese
Marcher à voile et à vapeur *[mahr-shee ah-vwahll-ee-ah-vah-per]*	**Bi** *[bee]*	バイ *[buy]*
Un(e) camé(e) *[ah cah-mee]*	**Lsd-junk** *[ehl-s-day joonk]*	麻薬常用者 *[mah-yah-koo-jo-yo-shah]*
Foutre la merde *[foo-tre lah merd]*	**Herrie schoppen** *[hehr-ree ss-chkop-ehn]*	トラブルメカ- *[toh-lah-boo-doo-meh-kah]*
Avec la tete aux nuages *[ah-vehc lah teht oh noo-ahsh]*	**Geflipt** *[chkeh-fleept]*	からっぽ頭 *[kah-lah-poh-ah-tah-mah]*
Un sac à vin *[ah sak ah vah]*	**Zuiplap** *[zaoop-lohp]*	アル中 *[ah-loo-choo]*
Mouche à merde *[moosh ah merd]*	**Geldwolf** *[chkeold-vohlf]*	インχキ弁護士 *[een-chee-kee behn-go-shee]*

English	Spanish	German
Ape shit *[ayp shiht]* To go crazy with anger. Lose temper.	**Cabreo** *[kah-bray-oh]*	**Ausser sich geraten** *[au-ser zeesh ger-a-ten]*
Armpit *[ahrm piht]* Derogatory for a place...i.e. We are in the armpit of th world.	**Barrio bajo** *[bah-rree-oh bah-khoh]*	**Am Arsch der Welt** *[am arsh der velt]*
Ass *[ahs]* A person whose behavior is silly and childish.	**Gilipollas, huevón** *[khee-lee-poh-yahss, weh-bon]*	**Arsch** *[arsh]*
Ass bandit *[ahss bahn-diht]* A gay person.	**Marica** *[mah-ree-kah]*	**Arschgeier** *[arsh-guy-yah]*
Ass-bite *[ahss-byt]* A general put-down for anyone who bothers you.	**Soplapollas** *[soh-plah-poh-yahss]*	**Arsch mit Ohren** *[arsh mit ohr-rehn]*
Asshole *[ahss-hohl]* An exceptionally stupid or obnoxious person.	**Pelotudo** *[peh-loh-too-doh]*	**Arschloch** *[arsh-loch]*

French	Dutch	Japanese
Péter un plomb *[pay-tee ah ploomb]*	**Witheet** *[veeht-hate]*	自我喪失 *[jee-gah so-shee-tzoo]*
Un trou à rat *[ah troo ah rah]*	**Goor hol** *[chkohr hohl]*	二次元 *[nee-jee-gen]*
Un cucul la praline *[ah koo-koo lah prah-leen]*	**Eikel** *[i-kohl]*	ばか *[bah-kah]*
Pédé *[pih-dee]*	**Flikker** *[fleeh-kerh]*	ホモ *[ho-mo]*
Un emmerdeur *[ah oh-meh-dir]*	**Veeg uit de pan** *[feh-ichk ah-oot deh pohn]*	うっとうしい奴 *[oot-toh-shee yah-tsoo]*
Un connard *[ah koh-nahr]*	**Oetlul** *[ooht-leh-ohl]*	あほんだらあ *[ah-hon-dah-lah]*

English	Spanish	German

Ass kisser
[ahss kih-ssehr]
Someone who
flatters a superior
with the hope of
future rewards.

Lame culos
[lah-meh koo-lohss]

Arschlecker
[arsh-lek-kah]

Artsy-fartsy
[ahr-tsee fahr-tsee]
Very pretentious.
Derogatory for
someone artisic.

Creído, -a
[kray-ee-doh, -dah]

Furzer
[fuhr-tzah]

Ask for it
[ahssk fohr iht]
Rationalization for
doing something
bad to someone
else. I.E., He
asked for a punch
in the face, so i
gave it to him.

**Estar
buscándolo**
*[ehs-tahrr booss-
kahn-doh-loh]*

**Darum
betteln**
[dar-room bet-teln]

Aussie
[owh-see]
A native of Austra-
lia.

Australiano,a
*[owhss-trah-lee-ah-
noh, -nah]*

Aussie
[aus-see]

Awesome
[awh-ssuhm]
Unbelievably great.
Excellent.

**De puta
madre**
*[deh poo-tah mah-
dreh]*

Affentittengeil
[af-fen-tit-ten-guyl]

French	Dutch	Japanese
Un lèche-cul *[ah lesh-koo]*	**Hielelikker** *[heehh-leh leeh-kerh]*	おべっか使い *[oh-beh-kah tsoo-kah-ee]*
Qui pète plus haut que son cul *[kee -peh-teh ploo oh ker sohn koo]*	**Kunstluis** *[koonst-laush]*	うぬぼれ屋 *[oo-noo-boh-reh yah]*
Chercher la merde *[shehr-shee la merd]*	**D'r om vragen** *[dehr ohm frah-chken]*	正当化 *[say-toh-kah]*
Un kangourou *[ah kohn-geh-roo]*	**Kangoeroe** *[kahn-chkoo-rooh]*	オストラリア人 *[oh-soo-toh-lah-lee-ah jeen]*
Génial *[gee-nee-al]*	**Te gek!** *[teh chkehk]*	抜群 *[bah-tsoo-goon]*

English	Spanish	German

Awol
[ay-wohl]
Absent without
leave. To be
missing.

Desertor, -a
[deh-sehrr-tor, -ah]

Fahnenflüchtig
[fahn-en-flish-tish]

Axe
[ahkss]
To fire someone or
to be fired (axed).

**Dar un
hachazo**
*[dahr oon ah-cha-
thoh]*

Jmdn. feuern
*[ye-man-den foy-
yern]*

French	Dutch	Japanese
S'être barré *[seh-treh bah-ray]*	**Met de noorderzon vertrokken** *[meht deh nohr-dehr-zohn vehr-troh-kehn]*	うわのそら *[oo-wah-no-so-lah]*
Viré *[vee-ray]*	**De zak geven/krijgen** *[deh zohk chkeh-ee-vehn/krah-ee-chkehn]*	くび *[koo-bee]*

B

is for...

Blowjob

English	Spanish	German

Babbler
[bahb-lehr]
Someone who has diahrea of the mouth. Canít stop talking.

Lora, cotorra
[loh-rah, koh-toh-rrah]

Laberer
[la-be-rah]

Backstabber
[bahk-sstahber]
A behind-your-back enemy.

Traidor
[trry-dohr]

Hinterfotziger
[hin-ter-fo-tzigah]

Backseat driver
[bahk-sseet dry-vehr]
Someone who has never driven, but knows how to drive the best.

Copiloto
[koh-pee-loh-toh]

Besserwisser
[bes-sah-vee-sa]

Bad
[bahd]
Very good.

Cojonudo
[koh-khoh-noo-doh]

Geil
[guyl]

Badass
[bahd-ahss]
Very, very good. A very tough person.

Chulo
[choo-loh]

Super Schwanz
[zoo-pah shv-ahnc]

Bad mouth
[bahd mowhth]
Spread negative opinions about someone or something.

Rajar
[rah-khar]

Klatschweib
[klatz-vibe]

French	Dutch	Japanese
Une pipelette *[oo-nah pee-pih-lett]*	Ouwehoer *[ah-oo-eh-hoorh]*	おしゃべり *[oh-shah-beh-lee]*
Un traitre *[ah treh-troo]*	Achterbaks *[achk-tehr-bahks]*	陰口野郎 *[kah-geh-goo-chee yah-low]*
Un co-pilote *[ah coh-pee-lot]*	(Niki) Lauda *[nee-kee lah-oo-dah]*	無免許野郎 *[moo-men-kyoh yah-low]*
Superbe *[soo-perb]*	Tof *[tohf]*	すごくいい *[soo-go-koo-ee]*
Un frimeur *[ah free-mer]*	Heftig *[hehf-tehchk]*	タフ *[tah-hoo]*
Casser *[keh-see]*	Achterklap *[achk-tehr-klohp]*	悪口 *[wah-loo-goo-chee]*

English	Spanish	German

Bag
[bahg]
An unnattractive woman.

Vomitiva
[voh-mee-tee-vah]

Gewitterziege
[ge-vee-ter-tzee-geh]

Bag it
[bahg iht]
To end or cancel a possible activity.

Corta el rollo
[kohr-tah ehl rroh-yoh]

Schluß machen
[shloos mah-ehn]

Bag lady
[bahg laydee]
A homeless lady.

Vagabunda
[bah-gah-boon-dah]

Pennerweib
[pen-uhr-vib]

Bagman
[bahg-mahn]
The person who collects the money in an illegal venture.

El recolector
[ehl rreh-koh-lehk-tor]

Abzocker
[ab-tzoh-kah]

Ball
[bawl]
To have sexual intercourse.

Meter mano
[meh-tehr mah-noh]

Pfefern
[feh-fehn]

Ballbreaker
[bawl-bray-kehr]
Give someone a hard time.

Jodón, rompe cojones
[kho-dohn, rohm-peh ko-kho-nehss]

Spielverderber
[shpeel-fuhr-der-bah]

Ballpark
[bawl-pahrk]
On average. In the vicinity.

Promedio
[proh-meh-dee-oh]

Bei den Leuten
[buy-den-loi-ten]

French	Dutch	Japanese
Gerbante *[ger-bont]*	**Koe** *[kooh]*	ブス *[boo-soo]*
Ferme-là! *[fehr-meur-lah]*	**Afzeggen** *[ohf-zeh-chkehn]*	中断 *[choo-dahn]*
Une clocharde *[oo-neh kloh-char-de]*	**Zwerfster** *[sz-vehr-rehf-stehr]*	浮浪者の女 *[hoo-low-shah no ohn-nah]*
Grabouilleur *[grah-boo-ee-ee-ehr]*	**Heler** *[heh-ee-lehr]*	賄賂受取人 *[wah-ee-loh oo-keh-toh-lee-neen]*
Baiser *[bih-zee]*	**Neuken** *[noh-oo-kehn]*	寝る *[neh-loo]*
Un emmerdeur *[oh mer-dehr]*	**Iemand het leven zuur maken** *[ee-mahndt heht leh-ee-vehn zoohr maah-kehn]*	雷おやじ *[kah-mee-nah-lee oh-yah-jee]*
Dans mon rayon *[don moh ray-yon]*	**Door de bank genomen** *[doohr deh bohnk chkehn-ohm-ehn]*	平凡 *[hay-bohn]*

English	Spanish	German

Balls
[bawlz]
Testicles.

Bolas,huevos, cojones,pelotas
[boh-lahss, weh-bohss, ko-kho-nehss, peh-loh-tahss]

Klöten
[kloo-ten]

Ballsy
[bawlzee]
Audacious.

Con cojones
[kohn ko-kho-nehss]

Rotzfrech
[rots-fresh]

Baloney
[bah-lowh-nee]
Nonsense, rubbish.

Bobada
[boh-bah-dah]

Kokolores
[ko-ko-lau-res]

Bananas
[bah-nahn-nahz]
Crazy.

Loco, -a
[loh-koh,-kah]

Deppert
[dep-pert]

Bang
[bayng]
To have sex with.

Tirar
[tee-rahr]

Es jmdm. geben
[es yeh-mahn-dem geb-ben]

Barf
[bahrf]
Vomit.Expression of disgust.

Vómitar
[voh-mee-tahr]

Kotz
[kohtz]

Bash
[bahsh]
A party. To criticize someone or something.

Criticar
[kree-tee-kahr]

Jmdn. einschüchtern
[yeh-mahn-den iyn-sush-tern]

French	Dutch	Japanese
Des couilles *[deh koo-yeh]*	**Kloten** *[kloat-ehn]*	金玉 *[keen-tah-mah]*
Avoir des couilles *[ah-vwah deh koo-yeh]*	**Lefgozerig** *[lehf-hoh-oo-szeh-reh]*	厚かましい *[ah-tsoo-kah-mah-shee]*
C'est une connerie *[see oo-nah con-ner-ree]*	**Lulkoek** *[leh-ohl koohk]*	戯言 *[tah-wah-go-toh]*
Dingue *[deng]*	**Gestoord** *[chkehs-tohrt]*	気違い *[kee-chee-gah-ee]*
Tirer son coup *[tee-reh sohn koo]*	**Kezen met** *[keh-ee-zehn meht]*	寝る *[neh-loo]*
Gerber *[geh-bee]*	**Kots** *[kohts]*	へど *[heh-doh]*
Une boum *[oo-neh boom]*	**Feessie** *[feh-ee-see]*	コンパ *[kohn-pah]*

English	Spanish	German
Basketcase *[bah-sskeht kayss]* Highly neurotic.	**Neura** *[neh-oo-rah]*	**Ein Fall für die Couch** *[iyn fahl fear dee coach]*
Bastard *[bah-sstahrd]* A jerk.	**Cabrón, bastardo** *[kah-brohn, bah-stahr-doh]*	**Bastard** *[bas-tard]*
Bat out of hell *[baht owht ahv hehl]* Extremely quick.	**Volando** *[voh-lahn-doh]*	**Rakete** *[rah-ket-teh]*
Batty *[baht-tee]* Strange.	**Raro, -a** *[rah-roh,rah]*	**Fremd** *[fre-hmd]*
Beat the meat *[beet thah meet]* Masturbation by hand (male).	**Hacerse una paja** *[ah-thehr-seh oo-nah pah-khah]*	**Wixen** *[veeks-ehn]*
Beaver *[bee-vehr]* Female genitalia.	**Coño** *[koh-nyoh]*	**Muschi** *[moo-shee]*
Beef *[beef]* *Complaint.*	**Queja** *[keh-khah]*	**Beschwerde** *[besh-fer-deh]*
Beefcake *[beef-kayk]* *Sexy guy*	**Papacito** *[pah-pah-thee-toh]*	**Sexy Rexy** *[sexy rexy]*

French	Dutch	Japanese
Un speedé *[ah spee-dee]*	**Zenuwelijer** *[zeh-ee-noo-veh-lahee-ehr]*	神経症の *[sheen-kay-sho no]*
Enculé! *[ohn-koo-lay]*	**Klootzak** *[klo-oo-tzack]*	あほ *[ah-ho]*
Un traçeur *[ah tra-sehr]*	**Vliegensvlug** *[fleeh-chkehn-shflechk]*	ぶっとばして *[boo-toh-bah-shee-teh]*
Zarbi *[zar-bee]*	**Maf** *[mohf]*	変人 *[hen-jeen]*
Une branlette *[oo-neh brau-lett]*	**Rukken** *[rooh-kehn]*	千ズリ *[sehn-zoo-lee]*
La foufounette *[lah foo-foo-net]*	**Pruimpje** *[prah-eem-pee-eh]*	オマンコ *[oh-mahn-koh]*
Une râlerie *[oo-neh-rah-leh-ree]*	**Gezeik** *[chkeh-zah-eek]*	ぐち *[goo-chee]*
Canon *[kah-non]*	**Lekker stuk** *[leh-kehr steck]*	色男 *[ee-low-oh-toh-koh]*

English	Spanish	German
Beerbelly [beehr-behl-lee] Huge stomach from drinking beer.	**Panza** [pahn- thah]	**Wanst** [vanst]
Behind [bee-hynd] Buttocks.	**Culo** [koo-loh]	**Tokus** [tuhk-koos]
Belly-laugh [behl-lee-lahff] Very loud laugh (i.e., Santa Claus).	**Carcajada** [kahr-kah-kha-dah]	**Bauchgröhlen** [bauch-grill-len]
Bender [behn-dehr] A long, long, long celebration involving alcoholic beverages or drugs.	**Juerga** [khwehr-gah]	**Ausschweifung** [aus-shvy-foong]
Bent behnt] Perverted.	**Pervertido, -a** [pehr-vehr-tee-doh, -dah]	**Pervers** [per-vers]
Big mouth [bihg mowth] Loud,vulgar person.	**Bocazas** [boh-kah-thahss]	**Schaumschläger** [shaum-shlay-gah]
Bigshot [bihg-shaht] Someone important.	**Engreido** [ehn-greh-ee-doh]	**Großkopfete** [gross-kop-fe-tuh]

French	Dutch	Japanese
Les abdo kronenbourg *[les ab-doh krohnen-boorg]*	**Vetzak** *[veht-zahk]*	ビ-ル腹 *[bee-loo bah-lah]*
Le popotin *[leu poh-poh-tah]*	**Kont** *[kohnt]*	尻 *[shee-lee]*
Un rire gras *[ah ree-rah grah]*	**Vette lach** *[veh-teh lochk]*	爆笑 *[bah-koo-show]*
Une orgie *[oon ohr-gee]*	**Slempartij** *[slehm-pahr-tie]*	大浮かれ *[oh-oo-kah-leh]*
Un vicelard *[ah vee-so-lahr]*	**Goor** *[chkohr]*	変質者 *[hen-shee-tsoo-shah]*
Une grande gueule *[ooh-neh gran-de girl]*	**Schreeuwlelijk** *[sjreh-oo-leh-ee-lehk]*	大口 *[oh-goo-chee]*
Un gros légume *[ah grow leh-goon]*	**Hoge piet** *[hoh-oochke peet]*	ビップ *[beep-poo]*

English	Spanish	German

Bimbo
[bihm-bowh]
Good looking,
dumb blond
(usually female)

Ricura
[ree-koo-rah]

Blondchen
[blond-shen]

Binge
bihnj]
To overindulge in
drinking, eating,
drugs, etc

Fartura
[fahr-too-rah]

Vielfraß
[feel-fras]

Bitch
[bihch]
Unpleasant woman,
i.e. Leona Helmsley
"The Queen of
Mean." To
complain exces-
sively, i.e. He
bitched and
moaned all night
about his job.

**Puta, perra,
zorra, guarra**
*[poo-tah, peh-rrah,
tho-rrah, gwah-rra]*

Hure
[hur-reh]

Bite me
[byt mee]
Fellaciate.Oh sure!
See "Suck my dick"

¡Chúpamela!
[choo-pah-meh-lah]

**Blas mir
einen**
[blass mee ai-nen]

Blah
[blah]
Very mediocre.

Una mierda
*[oo-nah mee-ehrr-
dah]*

Man so lala
[man zo lah-lah]

Blast
[blahsst]
A wild party.

Juerga
[khwehr-gah]

Exzeß
[ex-sess]

French	Dutch	Japanese
Une minette *[oo-neh mee-nett]*	**Blondje** *[bloh-een-deeh-eh]*	見かけのいい女 *[mee-kah-keh-no ee ohn-nah]*
S'éclater *[see-kleh-tee]*	**Slempen** *[ss-lehm-pehm]*	どんちゃん騒ぎ *[dohn-chahn-sah-wah-gee]*
Une salope *[oo-neh sah-lowp]*	**Kutwijf** *[koot-vah-eef]*	アバズラ *[ah-bah-zoo-lah]*
Fais-moi une gâterie *[feh-mwa oo-neh gah-tree]*	**Lik m'n reet** *[leek mehn hreh-eet]*	吸って *[soo-teh]*
Nul *[nool]*	**Minnetjes** *[meeh-neh-tshehs]*	くだらない *[koo-dah-lah-nah-ee]*
Un délire *[ah dee-lee-yah]*	**Knalfeest** *[k-nohl-feh-eest]*	ばか騒ぎ *[bah-kah-sah-wah-gee]*

English	Spanish	German

Blasted
[blah-sstihd]
Inebriated.

Estar pedo
[ehss-tahr peh-doh]

Kaput
[ka-poot]

Blooper
[bloo-pehr]
A mistake or
embarassing
expression.

Meter la pata
[meh-tehr lah pah-tah]

Lapsus
[lap-soos]

Blow job
[blowh jahb]
Fellatio.

Mamada
[mah-mah-dah]

Einen runter
holen
[ai-nen roon-tah hole-len]

Blue collar
[bloo kah-lehr]
Someone who
works at very
physical jobs,
working class.

Obrero
[oh-breh-roh]

Blaumann
[blau-man]

Bone-head
[bowhn-hehd]
A stupid person.

Idiota
[ee-dee-oh-tah]

Depp
[dehp]

Boner
[bowh-nehr]
An erection.

Ponerse dura,
empalmado
[poh-nehr-seh doo-rah, ehm-pahl-mah-doh]

Ein Harter
[ain har-tah]

Bonkers
[bahn-kehrz]
Go crazy.

Alocarse
[ah-loh-kahr-seh]

Verrückt
werden
[fehr-rikt ver-den]

Bonked
[bahnkt]
Expression for
sexual intercourse.

Culear
[koo-leh-ahr]

Bumsen
[boom-zen]

French	Dutch	Japanese
Bourré *[boo-ray]*	**Lam** *[lohm]*	酔っ払い *[yoh-pah-lah-ee]*
Une bourde *[oo-neh boord]*	**Foutje** *[fah-oot-jeh]*	大間違い *[oh-mah-chee-gah-ee]*
Une pipe *[oo-neh peep]*	**Pijpen** *[pah-ee-pehn]*	フェラχオ *[feh-lah-chee-oh]*
Un prolo *[ah proh-low]*	**De gewone man** *[deh chkeh-voh-oon-eh mahn]*	ブルカラ- *[boo-loo-kah-lah]*
Une tête de noeud *[oon teht deu neu]*	**Idioot** *[ee-dee-oh-oot]*	間抜け *[mah-noo-keh]*
La trique *[lah treek]*	**Stijve** *[stah-ee-veh]*	へま *[heh-mah]*
Dingo *[dehn-go]*	**Geflipt** *[chkeh-fleept]*	気が狂う *[kee-gah koo-loo-oo]*
S'est fait sauté(e) *[see feh so-tee]*	**Wippen** *[veh-pehn]*	寝る *[neh-loo]*

English	Spanish	German
Boobs [boobz] Breasts.	**Tetas, peras** [teh-tahss, peh-rahss]	**Paradiesäpfel** [pah-rah-dees-ep-fell]
Boob tube [boob toob] Television.	**Tele** [teh-leh]	**Glotze** [glo-tzeh]
Booby-hatch [boo-bee-hahch] Mental institution.	**Manicomio, loquero** [mah-nee-koh-mee-oh, loh-keh-roh]	**Klapsmühle** [klaps-muh-le]
Booger [buh-gehr] Nose mucus.	**Moco** [moh-koh]	**Popel** [pop-el]
Boom box [boom bahkss] Very large radio.	**Loro, estereo** [loh-roh, ehss-teh-reh-oh]	**Sehr großes Radiogerät** [zer gross-ses rah-dee-oh-ger-rett]
Boondocks [boon-dahkss] Obscure place.	**En el quinto coño** [ehn ehl keen-toh oh-nyoh]	**Unheimlicher Ort** [oon-heim-lish-ah ort]
Boot [boot] Get rid of, kick out, dismiss (get the boot).	**Botar** [boh-tahr]	**Rausschmeißen** [raus-shmiy-sen]
Booze [booz] Alcholic beverage.	**Trago** [trah-goh]	**Gesöff** [geh-zoof]

French	Dutch	Japanese
Les nichons *[leh nee-shon]*	**Tieten** *[teet-tehn]*	おっぱい *[oh-pah-ee]*
La boîte *[lah bwot]*	**Buis** *[bah-uhsh]*	テレビ *[teh-leh-bee]*
Chez les dingues *[shay leh deng]*	**Gekkenhuis** *[chkeh-kehn-hah-ush]*	精神病院 *[say-sheen-byoh-een]*
La morve *[la morv]*	**Pulkje** *[pehl-kee-eh]*	鼻蕉 *[hah-nah-gee-loo]*
Un booster *[ah boo-ster]*	**Ghetto blaster** *[geh-to blas-tehr]*	でかラジ *[deh-kah-lah-gee]*
Trifouilly-les-Oies *[tree-foo-yee-lee-zoo-ah]*	**Hol** *[hohl]*	ジャングル *[john-goo-roo]*
Virer *[vee-ray]*	**De bons geven** *[deh bohnsh chkeh-ee-vehn]*	くび *[koo-bee]*
La picole *[lah pee-kohl]*	**Neut** *[neh-oot]*	酒 *[sah-keh]*

English	Spanish	German

Boozer
[boo-zehr]
Alcoholic.

Alcohólico
[ahl-koh-hoh-lee-koh]

Säufer
[zoy-fah]

Bop the baloney
[bahp thah bah-lowh-nee]
Male masturbation.

Menearsela
[meh-neh-ahr-seh-lah]

Onanieren
[o-nan-near-en]

Boff
bahff]
Have sex.

Follar
[foh-yahrr]

Geschlecht-verkehr ausüben
[geh-shlesht-fehr-ker aus-ee-ben]

Bozo
[boh-zoh]
A clown.

Payaso
[pah-yah-soh]

Clown
[clown]

Broad
[brawhd]
A vulgar woman.

Pedorra
[peh-doh-rrah]

Vulgärin
[vul-ger-een]

Broke
[brohk]
To run out of money (empty pockets).

Estar sin un chavo
[ehss-tahr seen oon chah-boh]

Pleite
[ply-teh]

Brownie points
[browh-nee poyntz]
Symbolic award one gets for impressing someone.

Premio
[preh-mee-oh]

Schönheits-preis
[shoon-hiytz-price]

French	Dutch	Japanese
Un alcolo *[oon ahl-koh-low]*	**Zuipert** *[zah-eep-ehrt]*	アル中 *[ah-loo-choo]*
La veuve poignée *[la verv poh-nyay]*	**Trekken** *[trehk-kehn]*	オナニ- *[oh-nah-neee]*
Tirer sa crampe *[tee-ray sah krohmp]*	**Bonken** *[bohn-kehn]*	セックスする *[seh-koo-soo soo-loo]*
Une pitae *[oon pee-tah]*	**Mafkees** *[mohf-keh-ees]*	道化師 *[doh-keh-shee]*
Une pétasse *[oonpee-tas]*	**Sletje** *[ss-leh-eet-jeh]*	ミろげる女 *[hee-roh-geh-loo ohn-nah]*
être fauché *[eh-twa foo-shay]*	**Pleite** *[plah-ee-teh]*	オケラ *[oh-kay-lah]*
Un bon point *[oon boon pwah]*	**Puntje** *[peh-oohn-t-jeh]*	賞 *[show]*

English	Spanish	German

Brown noser
[browhn noh-zer]
Someone who goes out of her way to be agreeable. I.e., have your nose stuck up someones ass.

Chupa medias
[choo-pah meh-dee-ahss]

Arschkriecher
[arsh-kree-shah]

Brown shower
[browhn showh-ehr]
The act of taking a shit on another during the act of Coprophilia.

Cagarse
[kah-gahrr-seh]

Kaviar
[kah-vee-ahr]

Brown sugar
[browhn shuh-gehr]
An attractive black woman.

Morochita
[moh-roh-chee-tah]

Brauner Zucker
[brow-nah tzoo-kah]

Buck
[buhk]
A dollar.

Peso
[peh-soh]

Knete
[kneh-teh]

Bull dyke
[buhl dyk]
A very masculine lesbian.

Machona
[mah-choh-nah]

Sehr masculine Lesbe
[zehr mas-koo-leen-eh lez-beh]

Bullshit
[buhl-shiht]
Expression to convey skepticism. Nonsense

Estupidez
[ehss-too-pee-deth]

Quatsch
[kvah-tsh]

French	Dutch	Japanese
Un lèche-bottes *[ah lesh bot]*	**Slijmbal** *[slime-ball]*	おべっか使い *[oh-beh-kah zoo-kah-ee]*
Scato *[ss-cah-toh]*	**Op iemand's kop schijten** *[ohp ee-mahnds khop schkah-ee-tehn]*	オシッコシャワ- *[oh-shee-koh-shah-wah]*
La belle noire *[la bel-leh noo-wahr]*	**Zwarte doos** *[zoo-ahr-teh dose]*	黒砂糖 *[koo-loh-zah-toh]*
Une balle *[oon bahl]*	**Piek** *[peek]*	1 ドル *[ee-chee-doh-loo]*
Une vrille *[oon vree]*	**Pot** *[poht]*	男役レズ *[dahn-yah-koo-leh-zoo]*
Du bidon *[doo bee-dohn]*	**Slap gelul** *[ss-lohp chkeh-lehl]*	ナンセンス *[nahn-sehn-soo]*

English	Spanish	German
Bum *[buhm]* Buttocks.	**Nalgas** *[nahl-gahss]*	**Gesäß** *[geh-zes]*
Bummer *[buhm-mer]* A disappointment.	**Desilusión** *[deh-see-loo-see-ohn]*	**Hammer** *[ham-mah]*
Buns *[buhnz]* Buttocks.	**Trasero** *[trah-seh-roh]*	**Arsch** *[arsh]*
Burn *[buhrn]* Take advantage or steal	**Chorizear** *[choh-ree-theh-ahr]*	**Brennen** *[breh-nen]*
Bush *[buhsh]* The hair on female genitalia.	**Pelambre, pendejos** *[peh-lahm-breh, pehn-deh-khos]*	**Busch** *[boosh]*
Bust *[buhsst]* Arrest. Breasts.	**Teteras** *[teh-teh-rahss]*	**Knast** *[knahst]*
Butch *[buhch]* Very masculine. Often used to describe certain homosexuals.	**Marimacho** *[mah-ree-mah-choh]*	**Macho** *[mah-cho]*
Butt *[buht]* Buttocks.	**Ancas** *[ahn-kahss]*	**Arsch** *[arsh]*

French	Dutch	Japanese
Le derrière *[leu de-ree-eyr]*	**Toges** *[toh-oo-chkesh]*	けつ *[keh-tsoo]*
Une tuile *[oon tweel]*	**Kut!** *[keht]*	期待外れ *[kee-tai-hah-zoo-leh]*
Fesses *[fehs]*	**Kadetten** *[kah-deht-tehn]*	しり *[shee-ree]*
Piquer *[pee-kay]*	**Jatten** *[yoht-tehn]*	ねこばば *[neh-koh-bah-bah]*
La touffe *[lah toof]*	**Oerwoud** *[oo-ehr-vah-oot]*	繁み *[shee-geh-mee]*
Serrer *[seh-hreh]*	**Ballen** *[bohl-lehn]*	逮捕 *[tah-ee-ho]*
Un hommasse *[oon oh-mahs]*	**Macho** *[mah-tcho]*	男勝り *[oh-toh-koh-mah-sah-lee]*
L'arrière-train *[lah-ree-eyr-trahn]*	**Reet** *[hreh-eet]*	しり *[shee-lee]*

English	Spanish	German

Butter up
[buht-tehr ahp]
To go out of the way to make someone feel good, usually someone you want to impress.

Lamer el culo
[lah-mehr ehl koo-loh]

Jmdm. Brei ums Maul schmieren
[yeh-man-dem brai-ooms mowl shmee-ren]

Buzz off
[buhz ahff]
Impolite way of saying please go away.

¡Lárgate!
[lahr-gah-teh]

Zieh Leine
[tsee-lai-neh]

French	Dutch	Japanese
Passer de la pommade *[pah-say deu lah poh-mahd]*	**Slijmen** *[ss-lah-ee-mehn]*	おべっかを使う *[oh-beh-kah wo-tsoo-kah-oo]*
Dégage! *[day-gaj]*	**Opzouten** *[ohp-zah-oo-tehn]*	あっちへ行け *[ah-chee-eh ee-keh]*

C

is for...

Creepy

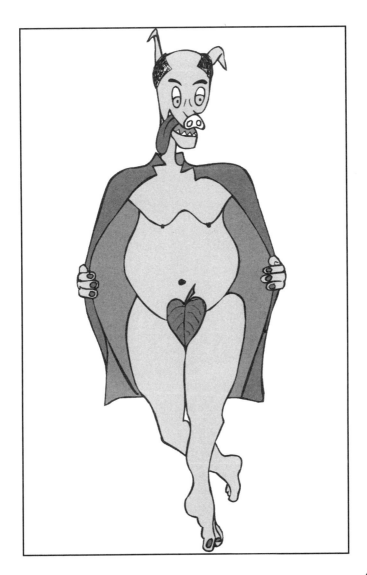

English	Spanish	German

Can
[kahn]
A toilet.

Cagadero
[kah-gah-deh-roh]

Pott
[pot]

Case
[kayss]
To inventory possessions with the intent to steal, i.e, to case the joint.

Evaluar la mercancía
[eh-vah-loo-ahr lah mehr-kahn-thee-ah]

Ein Objekt im Hinblick auf einen beabsichtigten Diebstahl hinunter- suchen
[ain oh-bee-yekt eem hin-bleek auf ai-nen beh-ab- zeesh-tee-gen deeb-shtahl hin oon-ter-zoo-chen]

Cat-house
[kaht-howhss]
A brothel.

Burdel
[boorh-dehl]

Puff
[poof]

Chassis
[chah-see]
Slang for an attractive womanís body.

Chasis
[chah-seess]

Fahrgestell
[fahr-geh-shtell]

Cheapskate
[cheep-sskayt]
A miser.

Tacaño
[tah-kah-nyoh]

Geizhals
[guyts-hals]

Cheesy
[chee-zee]
Inferior, poorly made goods. Silly, stupid and con- trived.

Cursi, huachafo
[koorh-see, wah- chah-foh]

Käse
[keh-zeh]

French	Dutch	Japanese
Les chiottes *[le shyoht]*	**Schijthok** *[ss-chka-eet-hok]*	便所 *[bahn-jo]*
Reperage *[reh-peh-hrash]*	**Proletarisch-boodschap-penlijstje** *[proh-oo-leh-tah-rish boh-ood-schkoh-pehn-lah-eesh-ee-eh]*	ちょんぼる *[chohn-boh-loo]*
Le lupanard *[le loo-pah-nahr]*	**Hoerekast** *[who-ehr-kahst]*	ソプランド *[soh-poo-lahn-doh]*
Une belle carrosserie *[oo-neh bell ka-ro-seu-ree]*	**Lekkertje** *[leh-kehr-tjeh]*	ナイスボディ *[nah-ee-soo-boh-dee]*
Un piscou *[ah peek-soo]*	**Lul-de-behanger** *[loohl-deh-beh-han-gehr]*	けち *[keh-chee]*
Breloque *[breu-lok]*	**Rotzooi** *[hroht-zoh-ee]*	安もん *[yah-soo-mohn]*

English	Spanish	German
Chick *[chihk]* A girl.	**Hembrita, tia** *[ehm-bree-tah, tee-ah]*	**Mädel** *[meh-del]*
Chicken hawk *[chih-kehn hawhk]* An older man who has a sexual interest in young boys.	**Pederasta** *[peh-deh-rah-stah]*	**Knabenschünder** *[knah-ben-shin-dah]*
Chicken shit *[chih-kehn shiht]* A coward.	**Cobarde** *[koh-bahr-deh]*	**Hosenscheißer** *[ho-zen-shiy-sah]*
Chill *[chihl]* Relax, donít get excited.	**¡Tranquilo, -a!** *[trahn-kee-loh, lah]*	**Immer mit der Ruhe** *[ihmah meet deh roowe]*
Chisel *[chih-zihl]* To cheat.	**Engañar** *[ehn-gah-nyahr]*	**Bescheißen** *[beh-shiy-sen]*
Choke *[chohk]* To fail at the most important moment.	**Cagarla al final** *[kah-ghahr-lah ahl fee-nahl]*	**Mit Pauken und Trompeten durchrasseln** *[mit pau-ken oond trum-pet-ten doorsh-raz-zeln]*
Chuck *[chuhk]* To vomit.	**Vomitar** *[voh-mee-tahr]*	**Kotzen** *[koh-tsen]*

French	Dutch	Japanese
Une nénette [oo-neh neh-net]	Wijf [vah-eef]	小娘 [koh-moo-soo-meh]
Un vieux pédé [ah veu peh-dee]	Pedo [peh-ee-doh]	ロリコン [loh-lee-kohn]
Une poule mouillée [oo-neh pool moo- yeh]	Lafbek [lohf-behk]	臆病者 [oh-koo-byoh-moh- no]
Cool [kool]	Rustig! [hroos-techk]	頭を冷やせ [ah-tah-mah-oh hee-yah-seh]
Truander [troo-an-deh]	Bedonderen [beh-dohn-deh- rehn]	ぺてん師 [peh-ten-shee]
Ne pas assurer [neu pah ah-soo- ray]	Afgaan als een gieter [ahf-chkahn ahls ehn chkit-ter]	だめにする [bah-meh-nee soo- loo]
Gerber [jer-bee]	Nekken [neh-khehn]	へどを吐く [heh-doh oh hah- koo]

English	Spanish	German
Chump *[chuhmp]* An easily fooled person.	**Pelmazo** *[pehl-mahl-thoh]*	**Trottel** *[tro-tell]*
Chutzpah *[khutz-pah]* To be insolent.	**Espabilado** *[es-pah-bee-lah-doh]*	**Frechheit** *[fresh-hite]*
Cig *[ssihg]* Abbreviation for cigarette.	**Pucho** *[poo-choh]*	**Kippe** *[kee-peh]*
Clap *[klahp]* Syphilis.	**La sifilítica** *[lah see-fee-lee-tee-kah]*	**Syph** *[zeeff]*
Clean out *[kleen owht]* To be robbed of everything.	**Desvalijar** *[dehss-vah-lee-khar]*	**Ausgenommen wie eine Weihnachts-gans** *[aus-geh-no-men vee ai-neh vai-nachts-gunz]*
Clinker *[kleen-kehr]* A flop.	**Un fracaso** *[oon frah-kah-soh]*	**Satz mit x,wir wohl nix** *[zats mit iks vear vohl nix]*
Clit *[kliht]* Clitoris.	**Clítoris** *[clee-toh-reess]*	**Kitzler** *[kitz-lah]*

French	Dutch	Japanese
Un nigaud *[ah nee-go]*	**Sufkop** *[soof-kohp]*	ばか *[bah-kah]*
Du culot *[doo koo-loh]*	**Grof in de bek** *[chkrohf ihn deh behk]*	元気 *[gen-kee]*
Une clope *[oo-neh clup]*	**Peuk** *[peh-ook]*	シガ- *[see-gah]*
La chaude-pisse *[la-shood-pees]*	**Syf** *[seeph]*	梅毒 *[bai-yee-doh-koo]*
Se faire plumer *[seu fehr ploo-may]*	**Kaalgeplukt** *[kaahl-chkeh-plookt]*	文無しになる *[moh-nah-shee nee nah-loo]*
Un flop *[ah flop]*	**Flop** *[flohp]*	へま *[heh-mah]*
Le clito *[loo-klee-toh]*	**Klitje** *[kliht-yeh]*	クリトリス *[koo-ree-toh-ree-soo]*

English	Spanish	German
Clobber [klah-behr] Beat someone up.	**Dar una paliza** [dahr oo-nah pah-lee-thah]	**Klopper** [klop-pah]
Clod [klahd] A clumsey person.	**Torpe** [tohr-peh]	**Plumpsack** [ploomp-zak]
Closet queen [klah-zeht kween] A secret homosexual.	**Maricona secreta** [mah-ree-koh-nah seh-kreh-tah]	**Hinterlader** [hin-ter-led-ar]
Cluck [kluhk] Dumb.	**Tarado, -a** [tah-rah-doh]	**Blöd** [bluud]
Cock [kahk] Penis.	**Polla** [poh-yah]	**Schwanz** [shvanz]
Cockamamie [kahk-ah-may-mee] An absurd idea.	**Ridiculez** [ree-dee-koo-leth]	**Eine absurde Idee** [ai-neh ab-sur-deh ee-day-yeh]
Cocksucker [kahk-suhk-ehr] A jerk.	**Chupapollas ; lameculos** [choo-pah-poh-yahss, lah-meh-koo-lohss]	**Blödmann** [bluud-mahn]

French	Dutch	Japanese
Tabasser *[tah-bah-say]*	**Afrossen** *[ahf-hroh-sehn]*	やってしまう *[yah-teh-shee-mah-oo]*
Un lourdaud *[ah loo-doh]*	**Kopkaas** *[kohp-kahs]*	のろま *[no-loh-mah]*
Un pédé non-déclaré *[ah peh-deh no-deh-klah-ray]*	**In de kast** *[ihn deh kahst]*	隠れホモ *[kah-koo-reh-ho-mo]*
Une gourde *[oo-neh gord]*	**Stompzinnig** *[ss-tohmp-zeen-echk]*	間抜け *[mah-noo-keh]*
La bite *[lah beet]*	**Lul** *[loohl]*	ちんぽ *[cheen-boh]*
Une idée à la mords-moi-le *[oo-neh ee-day a la mohr-mwa-leu]*	**Gelul** *[chkeh-loohl]*	馬鹿げた *[bah-kah-geh-tah]*
Une suceuse de bite *[oon soo-seus de beet]*	**Hondekop** *[hoohn-deh-kohp]*	吸い魔 *[soo-ee-mah]*

English	Spanish	German
Cockteaser *[kahk-tee-zehr]* A female who excites a man, but has no intention of having sexual intercourse..	**Calientahue-vos** *[kah-lee-ehn-tah-weh-bohss]*	**Schwanzhäns-lerin** *[shvanz-hens-leh-rin]*
Coke *[kohk]* Abbreviation for Cocaine.	**Coca ,penca, perico** *[koh-kah, pehn-kah, peh-ree-koh]*	**Schnee** *[shnee]*
Cold cock *[kohld kahk]* To knock someone unconscious.	**Hostia** *[ohss-tee-ah]*	**Kalt erwischen** *[kalt er-vee-shen]*
Cold turkey *[kohld tuhr-kee]* To quit a habit, such as smoking, drinking or drugs, suddenly.	**Cortar** *[kohr-tahr]*	**Plötzliche Abstinenz** *[ploots-lee-sheh ab-stee-nens]*
Collar *[kahl-lahr]* Police arrest.	**Enchironar** *[ehn-chee-roh-nahr]*	**Cafe Viereck** *[cafe fear-ek]*
Come *[kuhm]* To have an orgasm.	**Correrse** *[koh-rrehr-seh]*	**Kommen** *[com-en]*

French	Dutch	Japanese
Une allumeuse *[oon ahl-loo-meurs]*	**Teaser** *[tee-sehr]*	じらし女 *[jee-lah-shee-ohn-nah]*
Le coke *[leh kohk]*	**Bolletje wit** *[bol-leht-tjeh viht]*	シロ *[shee-loh]*
Envoyer au tapis *[ah-voy-yeh oh tah-pee]*	**Buiten westen slaan** *[bah-oo-tehn vehs-tehn slaahn]*	知らない間にノック *[shee-lah-nah-ee-mah-nee no-koo]*
Le sevrage *[leu sir-vraj]*	**Cold turkey** *[cohld tehr-key]*	禁酒、禁煙 *[keen-shoo keen-ehn]*
Embarquer *[em-bar-kay]*	**In de kraag grijpen** *[ihn deh krachk chkrrah-ee-pehn]*	逮捕 *[tah-ee-ho]*
Jouir *[shoo-eehr]*	**Spuiten** *[ss-pah-oo-tehn]*	いく *[ee-koo]*

English	Spanish	German

Con
[kahn]
Someone who has
spent time in jail..
Short for convict.

Ex-convicto
[ehkss-kohn-veek-toh]

Gauner
[gau-nah]

Conk
[kahnk]
The process by
which black people
straighten their
hair.

**Alisarse el
pelo**
[ah-lee-sahr-seh ehl
peh-loh]

Haare glätten
[ha-reh glet-ten]

Connect
[kuhn-nekt]
To have a meeting
of the minds.

**Estar en
sintonía**
[ehss-tahr ehn seen-toh-nee-ah]

**Sich auf
geistiger
Ebene
begegnen**
[zish auf guy-stee-geh
eh-beh-neh beh-geg-nen]

Cool
[koohl]
Very good, bohe-
mian.

**Genial,
cojonudo**
[gheh-nee-ahl, koh-khoh-noo-doh]

Cool
[kool]

Cootie
[koo-tee]
Nose mucus or an
imaginary disease
that kids pretend
oneanother have
upon any sort of
physical contact
with the opposite
sex.

Moco
[moh-koh]

Popel
[poh-pell]

French	Dutch	Japanese
Un taulard *[ah toh-lahr]*	**Bajesklant** *[bah-ees-kohnt]*	前科者 *[zen-kah-mo-no]*
Défriser *[de free-zeh]*	**Straighten en relaxen** *[ss-tray-tehn ehn hreh-laks-ehn]*	コンク *[kohn-koo]*
être sur la même longueur d'ondes *[eh-treuh soor la mem loon-ger dohnd]*	**Sporen** *[ss-poh-hrehn]*	透視 *[toh-shee]*
Le pied *[leu pee-yay]*	**Cool** *[koohl]*	クール *[koo-loo]*
La gale *[lah gahl]*	**Snot** *[ss-noht]*	えんがちょ *[en-gah-cho]*

English	Spanish	German
Cooter *[koo-tehr]* Vagina.	**Chucha, chocho** *[choo-chah, choh-choh]*	**Fotze** *[foh-tseh]*
Cop *[kahp]* Police officer.	**Madero, tombo** *[mah-deh-roh, tohm-boh]*	**Bulle** *[boo-leh]*
Copacetic *[koh-pa-sseh-tihk]* Allís well.	**¡De puta madre!** *[deh poo-tah mah-dreh]*	**Alles palletti** *[ah-less pah-let-tee]*
Couch potato *[kowch poh-tay-toh]* Someone whose primary hobby is sitting and watching television.	**Teleadicto** *[teh-leh-ah-deek-toh]*	**Sesselfurzer** *[zes-sell-foor-tsah]*
Cow *[kowh]* An ugly woman.	**Vaca** *[vah-kah]*	**Alte Küh** *[al-teh koo]*
Crack *[krahk]* An inexpensive and highly addictive form of cocaine.	**Pasta, pie** *[pahss-tah, pee-eh]*	**Crack** *[krahk]*
Crackpot *[krahk-paht]* Peculiar, bizarre person.	**Rarito, -a** *[rah-ree-toh]*	**Kauz** *[kautz]*

French	Dutch	Japanese
La chatte *[la shot]*	**Natte enveloppe** *[noht-teh ehn-vehl-ohp]*	χ ツ *[chee-tsoo]*
Un poulet *[oon poo-leh]*	**Smeris** *[ss-mee-hresh]*	サツ *[tsah-tsoo]*
ça baigne! *[sah beh-nyeh]*	**Picobello** *[pee-coh-beh-loh]*	良好 *[lyoh-koh]*
Un rantouflard *[oon rah-too-flahr]*	**Televisieziek** *[teh-leh-vee-see-zeek]*	テレビお宅 *[teh-leh-bee-oh-tah-koo]*
Une trume *[oo-neh troom]*	**Heks** *[hehcks]*	ぶさいく *[boo-sah-ee-koo]*
Crack *[khr-ahck]*	**Crack** *[krahk]*	コカイン *[koh-kah-een]*
Un cinglé *[ah sahn-glee]*	**Malloot** *[mah-loht]*	風変わり *[hoo-gah-wah-lee]*

English	Spanish	German
Cradle robber *[kray-duhl rah-behr]* An older man or woman who has a relationship with someone much younger.	**Viejo verde** *[vee-eh-khoh vehr-deh]*	**Alte Schachtel** *[al-teh shach-tel]*
Crap *[krahp]* To defecate.	**Cagarse** *[kah-gahr-seh]*	**Scheißen** *[shais-sen]*
Crash *[krahsh]* To sleep. Often, spending the night on someoneís couch.	**Quedarse frito** *[keh-dahr-seh free-toh]*	**Pennen** *[pen-nen]*
Cream *[kreem]* When a man feels sexually attracted to someone. Semen.	**Mojarse** *[moh-khahr-seh]*	**Sperma** *[sperm-mah]*
Creepy *[kree-pee]* Weird and strange.	**Siniestro** *[see-nee-ehss-troh]*	**Unheimlich** *[uhn-heim-lish]*
Croak *[krohk]* To die.	**Palmarla** *[pah-mahr-lah]*	**Abnippeln** *[ab-neep-peln]*

French	Dutch	Japanese
Un vieux marcheur *[ah vyeu mar-shehr]*	Pedo *[peh-ee-doh]*	ロリコン *[loh-lee-kohn]*
Chier *[shyay]*	Bouten *[bah-oo-tehn]*	きばる *[kee-bah-loo]*
Roupiller *[roo-pee-yeh]*	Maffen *[mohf-fehn]*	居眠り *[ee-neh-moo-lee]*
Bander à mort *[bon-deh ah mohr]*	Geil *[chkehl]*	でそう *[deh-soh]*
Bizarre *[bee-zar]*	Bizar *[bee-zahr]*	変人 *[hen-geen]*
Claquer *[klah-kay]*	De pijp uitgaan *[deh paeep ah-oot-chkahn]*	おだ仏 *[oh-dah-boo-tsoo]*

English	Spanish	German

Crook
[kruhk]
A criminal.

Delincuente
[deh-lee-kwehn-teh]

Gauner
[gow-nah]

Crow
[kroh]
Old and ugly
woman.

Vieja
[vee-eh-khah]

Alte Krähe
[al-teh kray-eh]

Crown jewels
[krowhn joo-ehlz]
A man's genitalia.

Cojones
[koh-khoh-nehss]

Kronjuwelen
[krohn-yoo-vehl-len]

Crud
[kruhd]
Filthy slime.

Mierda
[mee-ehrr-dah]

Rotz
[rots]

Cruise
[krooz]
Follow someone
with the desire to
engage in a sexual
encounter.

Ligar
[lee-gahr]

**Auf jmdn.
abfahren**
*[auf yeh-man-den
ab-fahr-ren]*

Crummy
[kruhm-mee]
Rotten.

Jodido
[kho-dee-doh]

Verkommen
[fehr-com-men]

Crush
[kruhsh]
A crowd as in a
party. Term for
being very at-
tracted to someone.

Flechazo
[fleh-chah-thoh]

Verknallt
[fehr-knalt]

French	Dutch	Japanese
Un(e) malhonnête *[ah mah-low-net]*	Boef *[boohf]*	犯人 *[hahn-neen]*
Une bique *[oo-neh beek]*	Ouwe taart *[ah-oo-eh taahrt]*	ばばあ *[bah-bah]*
Les bijoux de famille *[leh bee-joo deu fah-mee-yeh]*	Kroonjuwelen *[kron-you-veh-ee-lehn]*	金玉 *[keen-tah-mah]*
Un fumier *[oon foo-mee-yeh]*	Slijm *[slime]*	ケケケ *[keh-keh-keh]*
Draguer *[drah-geh]*	Cruising *[kroohs-ing]*	ナンパ *[nahn-pah]*
Crasseux *[krah-seu]*	Noten *[no-oo-tehn]*	腐った *[koo-sah-tah]*
Se toquer de quelqu'un *[seu toh-kay deu kel-kah]*	Lekkere gozer *[leh-keh-kre chkoh-oo-zehr]*	大パ-テイ- *[dah-yee-pah-tee]*

English	Spanish	German

Cunt
[kuhnt]
Female genitalia.
Derogatory term for
a woman.

Coño
[koh-nyoh]

Fotze
[foh-tseh]

French	Dutch	Japanese
La chatte *[lah shot]*	**Muts** *[moots]*	オマンコ *[oh-mahn-koh]*

D

is for...

Dead Head

English	Spanish	German

Dago
[day-goh]
Ethnic slur for someone of Italian descent.

Tano
[tah-noh]

Itaker
[ee-tak-ah]

Dame
[daym]
A common woman.

Chava
[chah-vah]

Tante
[tan-teh]

Damn
[dahm]
Abbreviation for God Dammit!

¡Joder!, ¡carajo¡
[kho-dehr, kah-rah-kho]

Verdammt
[fehr-damt]

Date rape
[dayt rayp]
Non-consentual sex between acquaintences.

Violada
[vee-oh-lah-dah]

Vergewaltigung unter Bekannten
[fehr-geh-val-tee-goong oon-tah beh-kan-ten]

Dead head
[dehd hehd]
Collequal term for a fan of the rock band The Greatful Dead, known for wearing tie-dyed clothing.

Progre
[proh-greh]

Dead Head
[ded hed]

Dead wood
[dehd wuhd]
Someone useless or superfluous

Inútil
[ee-noo-teel]

Tote Hose
[to-teh ho-zeh]

French	Dutch	Japanese
Un(e) rital(e) *[ah ree-tal]*	**Spaghettivreter** *[ss-pah-geh-tee-vreh-ee-tehr]*	イタリア人 *[ee-tah-lee-yah-jeen]*
Une gonzesse *[oon gohn-zes]*	**Sufkut** *[ss-ehf-keht]*	ありふれた女 *[ah-lee-hoo-leh-tah ohn-nah]*
Nom d'un chien! *[nom deh shyen]*	**Godver** *[chkod-fehr]*	畜生 *[chee-koo-sho]*
Un viol en rancard *[ah vee-ohl ohn rohn-kahr]*	**Weekendver-krachter** *[vee-kehnd-fehr-krachk-tehr]*	内輪レイプ *[oo-chee-wah-lay-pooh]*
Dead head *[dehd ehd]*	**Dead head** *[dehd-hehd]*	ロック *[loh-koo]*
Un boulet *[ah boo-lay]*	**Oen** *[oohn]*	役たたず *[yah-koo-tah-tah-zoo]*

English	Spanish	German
Deck *[dehk]* To punch someone.	**Meter una hostia** *[meh-tehr oo-nah ohss-tee-ah]*	**Jmdn. vermöbeln** *[yeh-man-den fehr-muh-beln]*
Deep six *[deep sihkss]* To get rid of someone or something.	**Cargarse a alguin** *[cahr-gahr-seh ah ahl-gee-ehn]*	**Jmdn. verlieren** *[yeh-man-den fehr-lee-rehn]*
Dick *[dihk]* Penis.	**Pinga, pichula** *[peen-gah, pee-choo-lah]*	**Schniedel-wutz** *[shnee-del-voots]*
Dick breath *[dihk brehth]* General insult.	**Come pollas** *[koh-meh poh-yahss]*	**Verunglimpf-ung** *[fehr-oon-gleemf-foonk]*
Dickhead *[dihk-hehd]* Stupid person.	**Cara polla** *[kah-rah poh-yah]*	**Holzkopf** *[holts-kopf]*
Dick-in-the-mouth *[dihk-ihn-thah-mowhth]* A general insult.	**Lame rabos** *[lah-meh rah-bohss]*	**Schmähung** *[shmeh-hoonk]*
Diddle *[dihd-duhl]* To have sex.	**Joder** *[kho-dehr]*	**Bohnern** *[bone-en]*

French	Dutch	Japanese
Envoyer (quelqu'un) au tapis *[on vwah-yeh oh tah-pee]*	**Rossen** *[hrohss-ehn]*	殴る *[nah-goo-roo]*
Balancer *[bah-loh-say]*	**Iemand lozen** *[ee-mahnd loh-oo-zehn]*	消す *[keh-soo]*
La queue *[la keu]*	**Pik** *[pehk]*	ちんぽ *[cheen-boh]*
Tete de noeud *[tehtd noo-ehd]*	**Ingeblikte kikker** *[ihn-chkeh-bleek-teh keeh-kehr]*	クソ野郎 *[koo-soh-yah-loh]*
Une tête de noeud *[oo-neh tayt deu neu]*	**Mafkees** *[mahf-keh-ees]*	馬鹿 *[bah-kah]*
Un espèce d'enculé! *[ah eh-spes dohn-koo-leh]*	**Hufter** *[hoof-tehr]*	あの野郎 *[ah-no-yah-loh]*
Baiser *[beh-zeh]*	**Teringlijer** *[teh-hring-lah-ee-ehr]*	寝る *[neh-loo]*

English	Spanish	German

Dime bag
[dym bahg]
$10 worth of drugs.

Talego
[tah-leh-goh]

Geldbeutel
[geld-boy-tel]

Ding-a-ling
[deeng-ah-leeng]
Penis or someone
who is foolish.

El penélope
*[ehl peh-neh-loh-
peh]*

Johannes
[yo-hahn-ess]

Dingbat
[deeng-baht]
A silly person.

Retrasado, -a
*[reh-trah-sah-doh, -
dah]*

Doofkopp
[doof-kop]

Dink
[deenk]
Ethnic slur for
person of Vietnam-
ese desent.

Chino, -a
[chee-noh, -nah]

Schlitzauge
[shlits-au-geh]

Dinky
[deen-kee]
Small.

Pequeño
[peh-keh-nyoh]

Winzig
[vin-sish]

Dipstick
[dihp-sstihk]
Insult for someone
stupid.

Tonto, -a
[tohn-toh, -tah]

Depp
[dep]

French	Dutch	Japanese
Une barrette (du haschish), une enveloppe (d'herbe) *[oo-neh bahr-rett, oo-neh ohn-veh-lope]*	**Tientje stuff** *[teen-tjeh ss-tooph]*	2グラム *[nee-goo-lah-moo]*
Le zizi *[leu zee-zee]*	**Hoerejong** *[whoo-hreh-yohng]*	ちんぽこ野郎 *[cheen-boh-koh-yah-loh]*
Une imbécile *[oo-neh em-beh-seel]*	**Puistekop** *[pah-ee-sst-eh-kohp]*	ぼけ *[boh-keh]*
Un chintoque *[ahn sheen-tohk*	**Pinda** *[peen-dah]*	ベトナム人 *[beh-toh-nah-moo-jeen]*
Trognon *[troh-nyohn]*	**Kleintje** *[klein-tje]*	ちよぼこい *[choh-boh-koy-yee]*
Con(nard) *[ko-nahr]*	**Imbeciel** *[ee-m-beh-seel]*	あほ *[ah-ho]*

English	Spanish	German
Dirt [duhrt] Gossip.	**Chisme** [cheess-meh]	**Gewäsch** [geh-vesh]
Dis [dihss] Slang for disrespect.	**Faltoso** [fahl-toh-soh]	**Respektlosigkeit** [reh-spect-low-zish-kite]
Dive [dyv] A disreputable bar or restaurant.	**Antro** [ahn-troh]	**Absteige** [ab-stuy-geh]
Do (the nasty) [doo-thah-nah-sstee] To have sex with.	**Joder** [kho-dehr]	**Über jmdn. rübersteigen** [e-ber yeh-man-den re-ber-stuy-gen]
Doobie [doo-bee] A joint.	**Porro, pito** [poh-rroh, pee-toh]	**Tüte** [tee-teh]
Doghouse [dohg-howhss] The place for someone who has been disgraced or humiliated.	**En la boca del lobo** [ehn lah boh-kah dehl loh-boh]	**Katzentisch** [kah-tsen-teesh]
Doll [dahl] Good looking woman.	**Muñeca** [moo-nyeh-kah]	**Püppchen** [poop-shen]

French	Dutch	Japanese
Des ragots *[deh rah-go]*	**Roddel** *[hroh-dohl]*	うわさ話し *[oo-wah-sah bah-nah-shee]*
Bêcher *[beh-cheh]*	**Min** *[mehn]*	失礼 *[shee-tsoo-lay]*
Un gargote *[ah gahr-goht]*	**Tent** *[tehnt]*	酒場 *[sah-kah-bah]*
Se la (le) faire *[seu lah fehr]*	**Het doen met** *[heht doohn meht]*	セックスする *[seh-koo-soo soo-roo]*
Un pétard *[ah peh-tahr]*	**Joint** *[joint]*	はっぱ *[hah-pah]*
Mis en côté *[mee ahn ko-tay]*	**In je mand!** *[ihn ee-eh mahnt]*	冷遇 *[lay-goo]*
Une poupée *[oo-neh poo-peh]*	**Schatje** *[ss-chkat-tee-eh]*	生かす女 *[ee-kah-soo-ohn-nah]*

English	Spanish	German
Dong [dahng] Penis.	**Salchichón** [sahl-chee-chohn]	**Stöpsel** [shteep-sel]
Dope [dohp] Drugs, particularly heroin.	**Heroína** [eh-roh-ee-nah]	**Dope** [dope]
Dork [dohrk] An undesirable man.	**Un pedo de tipo** [oon peh-doh deh tee-poh]	**Rüpel** [roo-pel]
Douchebag [doosh-bahg] Someone undesirable.	**Un pedo** [oon peh-doh]	**Lästige Setzkartoffel** [le-stee-geh zehts-kar-to-fehl]
Downer [dow-nehr] Something disappointing.	**Downer** [dow-oo-ner]	**Tiefschlag** [teef-shlok]
Drag [drahg] To dress in womenís clothing.	**Travestirse** [trah-vehss-teerh-seh]	**Sich tuntig kleiden** [zeesh toon-teesh kluy-den]
Drag queen [drahg kween] Homosexual transvestites.	**Travesti** [trah-vehss-tee]	**Tunte** [toon-teh]

French	Dutch	Japanese
Le gland *[leh glah]*	**Piemel** *[pee-eh-mehl]*	ペニス *[peh-nee-soo]*
Le dope *[leh dohp]*	**Dope** *[dope]*	ヤク *[yah-koo]*
Un crétin *[ah cray-tehn]*	**Engerd** *[ehn-gehrd]*	いやな奴 *[ee-yah-nah-yah-tsoo]*
Un(e) chieur(se) *[ah shee-yeur]*	**Griezel** *[chkreeh-zehl]*	たまらん奴 *[tah-mah-lahn-yah-tsoo]*
ça a foiré! *[sah ah fwah-ray]*	**Zak** *[zahk]*	最低 *[sah-yee-tay-yee]*
En travelo *[eun trah-veh-low]*	**Drag** *[drag]*	男の女装 *[oh-toh-koh no jo-soh]*
Une folle *[oon fohl]*	**Drag queen** *[drahg kween]*	おかま、おなべ *[oh-kah-mah oh-nah-beh]*

English	Spanish	German
Dreck [drehk] Garbage.	**Basura** [bah-soo-rah]	**Müll** [muhl]
Drop a dukey [drahp ah doo-kee] To defecate.	**Irse de cámaras** [eerh-seh deh kah-mah-rahss]	**Ein Ei legen** [ain iy leh-gen]
Dross [drahss] Excess and waste.	**Exceso** [ehkss-theh-soh]	**Verschwen-dung** [fehr-shven-doong]
Dry fuck [dry fuhk] Premature sex.	**Joder sin correrse** [kho-dehr seen koh-rrehr-seh]	**Kindersex** [keen-der-sex]
D.T.s [dee-teez] The process of withdrawal from alcohol or drugs. Abbreviation for delirium tremens.	**El mono** [ehl moh-noh]	**Gilb** [geelb]
Dukey [doo-kee] Defecation.	**Mierda** [mee-ehrr-dah]	**Scheiße** [shiy-seh]
Dude [dood] A cool guy.	**Tronco, tio** [trohn-koh, tee-oh]	**Coolmann** [cool man]

French	Dutch	Japanese
Du gnognot(te) *[doo nyoh-nyoh]*	**Vulles** *[veh-lehs]*	ごみ *[goh-mee]*
Débourrer *[deh-boo-ray]*	**Kakken** *[koh-kehn]*	うんちする *[oon-chee soo-loo]*
Le gaspi *[leu gah-spee]*	**Over de balk smijten** *[over deh bohlk ss-mah-ee-tehn]*	屑 *[koo-zoo]*
L'enfilage à sec *[lohn-fee-lah-jeh ah sehk]*	**Droogneuken** *[drah-oochk-neh-oo-kehn]*	ルセックス *[boo-loo-seh-koo-soo]*
Digue-digues *[deeg-deeg]*	**D.t.** *[day-tay]*	精神錯乱 *[say-sheen-sah-koo-lahn]*
Chier *[shee-eh]*	**Drol** *[dhrohl]*	うんこ *[oon-koh]*
Mec *[mek]*	**Gozer** *[chkoh-oo-zehr]*	洒落た男 *[shah-leh-tah-oh-toh-koh]*

English	Spanish	German
Dump [duhmp] A decrepit place. To defecate. To leave someone with whom you are having a relationship.	**Cagon** [kah-gohn]	**Jmdn. fallen lassen** [yeh-man-den fahl-len las-sen]
Dweeb [dweeb] A person who evokes contempt.	**Imbecil** [eem-beh-theel]	**Asozialer** [ah-sots-yah-lah]
Dyke [dyk] A lesbian.	**Lesbiana** [lehz-bee-ah-nah]	**Lesbe** [les-beh]

French	Dutch	Japanese
(noun) - **Un taudi** *[ah toh-dee]* (verb) - **Larguer** *[lah-geh]*	**Dumpen** *[dehm-pehn]*	捨てる *[soo-teh-loo]*
Une nouille *[oo-neh noo-ee]*	**Doppie** *[doh-pee]*	脱落者 *[dah-tsoo-lah-koo- shah]*
Une gouine *[oo-neh gween]*	**Potje** *[poh-tje]*	レズ *[leh-zoo]*

E

is for...

Egghead

English	Spanish	German
Eat her out *[eet hehr owht]* Perform cunnilingus.	**Comérsela** *[koh-mehr-seh-lah]*	**Leck sie** *[lek see]*
Eat me *[eet mee]* An insult that involves fellatio and implies a total disregard for the other person.	**¡Mámamela!** *[mah-mah-meh-lah]*	**Leck mich** *[lek mish]*
Eat my dust *[eet my duhsst]* An Insult that is often heard at road races.	**Traga polvo** *[trah-gah pohl-voh]*	**Friß meinen Staub** *[frees mai-nen shtaub]*
Ecch *[ehkh]* Expression of disgust.	**¡Puah!** *[pwah]*	**Bäh** *[beh]*
Egghead *[ehg-hehd]* Someone who reads and studies excessively. Too intelligent .	**Cabeza de huevo** *[kah-beh-tha deh weh-boh]*	**Eierkopf** *[Ai-yer-kopf]*
Endo *[ehn-doh]* Marijuana.	**Grifa, maría** *[gree-fah, mah-ree-ah]*	**Gras** *[grass]*

French	Dutch	Japanese
Sucer quelqu'un *[soo-seh kehl-kahn]*	Beffen *[beh-fehn]*	なめる *[nah-meh-loo]*
Mords-le-moi! *[mohr-leu-mwah]*	Kus m'n kont *[koosh mehn kohnt]*	私を食べて *[wah-tah-shee-oh tah-beh-teh]*
Mord ma poussière! *[mohrd mah poo-see-yehr]*	Krijg de tyfus *[khra-ee-chk deh tee-phoos]*	のろま *[no-lo-mah]*
Berk! *[behr]*	Getver *[chkeht-fehr]*	うえ- *[oo-eh]*
Un pollard *[ah poh-lahrd]*	Studentje *[ss-too-dehn-tje]*	インテリ *[een-teh-lee]*
L'herbe *[lhehrb]*	Stuff *[ss-tehf]*	マリファナ *[mah-lee-fah-nah]*

English	Spanish	German
Excellent *[ehkss-ssah-lehnt]* Really great.	**De puta madre** *[deh poo-tah mah-dreh]*	**Super** *[zoo-pah]*

French	Dutch	Japanese
Canon *[kah-nohn]*	**Onwijs** *[ohn-vah-ees]*	最高 *[sai-koh]*

F

is for...

Fuck

English	Spanish	German

Fab
[fahb]
Wonderful,
fabulous.

Super
[soo-pehr]

Toll
[tohl]

Faggot
[fahg-giht]
Slur for male
homosexual.

Mariposón
[mah-ree-poh-sohn]

Tunte
[toon-teh]

Fag hag
[fahg-hahg]
Woman who
befriends male
homosexuals.

Loca
[loh-kah]

Schwulentussi
[shfoo-len-too-see]

Fairy
[fayr-ree]
Slur for male
homosexual.

**Sostén finge
tetas**
[soh-stehn feen-geh
teh-tahss]

Bloud
[blowd]

Falsies
[fahl-seez]
Stuffing bra to
make breasts
appear larger.

**Tirarse un
pedo, un
cuesco**
[tee-rahrr-seh oon
peh-doh, oon
kwehss-koh]

Wonder-Bra
[vun-der brah]

Fart
[fahrt]
To break wind.

Tragar
[trah-gahr]

Furz
[foor-ts]

Feed bag
[feed-bahg]
To eat a lot (put on
the feed bag)

Mercachiflero
[mehr-kah-chee-
fleh-roh]

Fresse
[freh-seh]

French	Dutch	Japanese
Sensass *[sohn-sas]*	**Wreed** *[vhreh-eeht]*	言うことなし *[yoo-koh-toh-nah-shee]*
Une tante *[oo-neh tahnt]*	**Flikker** *[flehk-kehr]*	ホモ *[ho-mo]*
Une porte tapettes *[oon-eh pohrt-tah-peht]*	**Nichtenmoeder** *[nichk-tehn-mood-ehr]*	ホモの女友達 *[ho-mo-no ohn-nah-toh-moh-dah-chee]*
Une tapette *[oo-neh tah-pet]*	**Nicht** *[nichkt]*	ゲイ *[gay]*
Des roberts de chez Michelin *[deh roh-beh deu shay meesh-lahn]*	**Kunstperen** *[koohnst-pee-hrehn]*	乳パット *[chee-chee-pah-toh]*
Un pet *[ah peh]*	**Een scheet laten** *[ehn ss-cheh-eet lah-tehn]*	へをこぐ *[heh-yoh-koh-goo]*
Glouton *[gloo-tohn]*	**Je vol vreten** *[ee-eh vohl vreh-ee-tehn]*	大食い *[oh-goo-ee]*

93

English	Spanish	German

Fence
[fehnss]
Someone who sells
stolen goods.

Testaferro
[tes-tah-fehr-roh]

Hehler
[heh-lah]

Finger
[feen-gehr]
Gesture using
middle finger to
express contempt.
To identify a
criminal.

**Hacer un
dedo**
*[ah-thehr oon deh-
doh]*

Stinkefinger
*[shtin-keh-feen-
geh]*

Flake
[flayk]
Someone who is
forgetful or
inconsiderate.

Falso
[fahl-soh]

**Zerstreuter
Professor**
*[tser-stroi-tah pro-
fes-sah]*

Flack
[flahk]
Derogatory for a
publicist.
Excessive criticism
or complaints.

Inpertinente
*[een-pehr-tee-nehn-
teh]*

Kritikaster
[kri-tee-kas-tah]

Flashback
[flahsh-bahk]
A spontainous
vision of the past; a
vivid memory from
an LSD trip.

Alucinación
*[ah-loo-thee-nah-
see-ohn]*

Trip
[treep]

French	Dutch	Japanese
Receleur *[reu-ceu-leur]*	**Heler** *[heh-ee-lehr]*	ストリトセラ- *[soo-toh-lee-toh-seh-lah]*
Faire un bras d'honneur à quelqu'un *[fehr ah brah doh-neur ah kel-kahn]*	**Lik m'n hol** *[lihk mehn hohl]*	中指 *[nah-kah-yoo-bee]*
Fada *[fah-dah]*	**Warhoofd** *[vaahr-hoo-oft]*	間抜け *[mah-noo-keh]*
Gratte-pappier *[ghraht-pah-pee-eh]*	**Pennelikker** *[peh-neh-leek-ehr]*	ヘボ記者 *[heh-boh-kee-shah]*
Un flashback *[ah flash-back]*	**Flashback** *[flashback]*	ヒカリ *[hee-kah-ree]*

English	Spanish	German

Flasher
[flahsh-ehr]
A man who exposes himself in public for sexual thrills.

Exhibicionista
[ehkss-ee-bee-see-oh-nee-stah]

Flitzer
[fleet-tsah]

Flatfoot
[flaht-fuht]
A police detective.

Madero, tombo
[mah-deh-roh, tohm-boh]

Plattfuß
[plat-foos]

Flea bag
[flee-bahg]
A cheap hotel.

Antro
[ahn-troh]

Kakerlakennest
[kock-er-lock-en-nest]

Flick
[flihk]
A film.

Peli
[peh-lee]

Streifen
[shtreiy-fen]

Flop
[flahp]
An unsuccessful activity, i.e. film, play or book.

Cara dura
[kah-rah doo-rah]

Flop
[flohp]

Flunk
[fluhnk]
To fail.

Fracasar
[frah-kah-sahr]

Auf die Schnauze fallen
[auf dee shnau-tseh fahl-len]

Fly by night
[fly by nyt]
An unstable or unreliable business or organization

Chapuza
[chah-poo-tha]

Grauzone
[grau-zo-neh]

French	Dutch	Japanese
Un satyre *[ah sah-teer]*	**Potloodventer** *[pot-loh-oot-vehn-tehr]*	見せ□ らかし屋 *[mee-seh-bee-lah-kah-shee-yah]*
Un poulet *[ah poo-lay]*	**Wout** *[vah-oot]*	マッポ *[mah-poh]*
Un asile de nuit *[ah ah-zeel deu neu-ee]*	**Achenebbisj hotel** *[achk-neh-besh hoh-tehl]*	安宿 *[yah-soo-yah-doh]*
Le ciné *[leu see-neh]*	**Filmpie** *[feelm-pee]*	映画 *[ay-gah]*
Une bide *[oo-neh beed]*	**Flop** *[flohp]*	失敗作 *[shee-pah-yee-sah-koo]*
Merder *[mair-dair]*	**Zakken** *[zah-kehn]*	失敗する *[shee-pah-yee soo-loo]*
Pas sérieux *[pa sai-ree-ou]*	**Een louche bedrijfje** *[ahn loosh beh-drah-ee-fee-eh]*	夜逃げ *[yo-nee-geh]*

English	Spanish	German

Foreskin
[fohr-sskihn]
That funny part of
an uncircumcised
dick.

Pellejo
[peh-yeh-kho]

Vorhaut
[for-chowt]

Four eyes
[fohr eiz]
Someone who wears
glasses.

Cuatro ojos
[kwah-troh oh-khohss]

Vier Augen
[fear ow-gen]

Fox
[fahkss]
Sexy woman.

Hembrón
[ehm-brohn]

Rasseweib
[ras-seh-vibe]

Freak
[freek]
Anyone who is
weird or unusual.

Monstruo
[mohn-stroo-oh]

Freak
[freek]

Freak out
[freek owht]
Go crazy.

Aterrorizarse
[ah-tehrr-oh-ree-thahr-seh]

Am Rädchen drehen
[am red-shen dray-yen]

Frog
[frohg]
Someone from
France.

Gabacho, -a
[gah-bah-choh, -chah]

Froschfresser
[frosh-fres-sah]

Fuck
[fuhk]
Sexual intercourse.

Follar, tirar
[foh-yahr, tee-rahr]

Fick
[fik]

French	Dutch	Japanese
Le prépuce *[lai prai- pis]*	Voorhuid *[voohr-ha-oot*	ふくろ *[hoo-koo-loh]*
Rinoclard *[ree-no-clarg]*	Brillejood *[bhreel-leh-ee-oh-oot]*	眼鏡小僧 *[meh-gah-neh-ko-zo]*
Un beau petit lot *[an boh paitee lo]*	Kanjer *[kahn-ee-ehr]*	エロい女 *[eh-lo-yee-ohn-nah]*
Un(e) original(e) *[an o-ree-gee-nal]*	Malloot *[mah-loh-oot]*	変人 *[hen-jeen]*
Flipper *[flee-paih]*	Uit je dak gaan *[ah-oot ee-eh dohk chkaahn]*	気が狂う *[kee-gah-koo-roo-oo]*
Quouillon(nne) *[cui-ion]*	Fransoos *[fhrahn-so-oos]*	フランス人 *[foo-lahn-soo jeen]*
Baiser *[bai-sai]*	Rampetampen *[hrahm-peh-tahm-pehn]*	やる *[yah-loo]*

English	Spanish	German

Fuck head
[fuhk hehd]
Complete idiot.

Oligofrénico, -a
[oh-lee-go-freh-nee-koh, -kah]

Vollidiot
[fall-id-i-ot]

Fuck off
[fuhk ahff]
Go away, donít bother me.

¡Lárgate!
[lahr-gah-teh]

Verpiß dich
[fer-pees deesh]

Fuck up
[fuhk uhp]
To make a mistake or beat up. A failure.

Cagarla
[kah-gahr-lah]

Leck mich doch am Arsch
[lehk meesh doch am arsh]

Funny farm
[fuhn-nee fahrm]
Mental institution.

Manicomio
[mah-nee-koh-mee-oh]

Klapsmühle
[klups-mueh-leh]

Fur burger
[fuhr buhr-gehr]
Derogatory word for a womanís vagina.

Almeja
[ahl-meh-khah]

Möse
[moo-zeh]

100

French	Dutch	Japanese
Un crétin *[ahn crai-tan]*	**Gestoorde** *[gehs-toohr-deh]*	白痴 *[hah-koo-chee]*
Va te faire foutre! *[vat fer foo-trh]*	**Sodemieter op!** *[soh-deh-mee-tehr-op]*	出ていかんかい *[deh-teh-ee-kahn-kai]*
Foutre la merde *[foo-trh lah maird]*	**Verkankeren** *[vehr-kahn-keh-rehn]*	へま *[heh-mah]*
Asile de dingues *[ah-seal daih dahng]*	**Gekkenhuis** *[chkeh-kehn-hah-oos]*	気違い病棟 *[kee-chee-gah-yee-byo-toh]*
Con *[cohn]*	**Doos** *[doh-oos]*	女のあそこ *[oh-nah no ah-so-koh]*

G

is for...
Geek

103

English	Spanish	German

Gaff
[gahff]
A social blunder.

Disparate
[dee-spah-rah-teh]

Fauxpas
[fowks-pas]

Gang bang
[gayng bayng]
When a group of
men have sex with
a woman.

Orgía
[ohr-ghee-ah]

Kegelclub
[kay-gel-kloob]

Gangbusters
[gayng-buh-sstehrz]
To do something
with great enthusi-
asm (Going like
gangbusters)

Marabunta
[mah-rah-boon-tah]

Besessenheit
[bes-seh-sen-height]

Gas
[gahss]
Fun. Bad smell from
someone breaking
wind.

Pedo
[peh-doh]

**Ein
Schirmchen**
[ain shirm-shen]

Gas guzzler
[gahss guhz-lehr]
A large automobile.

Barco
[bahr-koh]

Benzinsäufer
[ben-zeen-zoi-fah]

Gay
[gay]
Homosexual.

Maricona
[mah-ree-koh-nah]

Schwul
[shfool]

French	Dutch	Japanese
Une gaffe *[oon-neh gahf]*	**Afgang** *[ahf-chkahng]*	とんま *[tohn-mah]*
Une baptême *[oon-neh bap-taih-maih]*	**Triootje** *[tree-oh-oo-tje]*	性交パ- テイ- *[say-koh-pah-tee]*
Faire la fête *[faihr la faih-teh]*	**We gaan ervoor** *[veh chkahn ehrh-vohr]*	熱くなる *[ah-tsoo-koo-nah-roo]*
Super *[soo-paihr]*	**Scheet** *[ss-chkeh-eet]*	へ *[heh]*
La bagnole *[lah bah-niohl]*	**Bak** *[bahk]*	アメ車 *[ah-meh-shah]*
Pédé *[paih-daih]*	**Homo** *[hoh-moh]*	ホモ *[ho-mo]*

English	Spanish	German
Geek [geek] A foolish person.. Originally someone at a freak show that bit the heads off chickens.	**Tonto, -a** [tohn-toh, -tah]	**Tölpel** [tool-pel]
Geezer [gee-zehr] An old man.	**Viejo** [vee-eh-kho]	**Alter Knacker** [al-tah kna-kah]
Get laid [geht layd] Have sexual intercourse.	**Acostarse con alguien** [ah-kohss-tahr-seh kohn ahl-gee-ehn]	**Jmdn. flach legen** [yeh-man-den flach leg-gen]
Get lost [geht lohsst] Go away.	**¡Piérdete!** [pee-ehr-deh-teh]	**Verschwinde** [fehr-shveen-deh]
Get out [geht owht] Expression of disbelief.	**¡Sal de aquí!** [sahl deh ah-kee]	**Hau ab** [how ub]
Ghetto-blaster [geht-toh-blah-sstehr] A large radio.	**Radio portátil** [rah-dee-oh pohr-tah-teel]	**Kasten** [kas-ten]
Gimp [gihmp] Someone who is crippled.	**Tullido, -a** [too-yee-doh, -dah]	**Krüppel** [krip-pel]

French	Dutch	Japanese
Un monstre *[ahn mauhn-stre]*	**Mafkees** *[mahf-keh-ees]*	うすのろ *[oo-soo-no-loh]*
Un vieux schnock *[ahn vee-eh ssh-knock]*	**Ouwe lul** *[ah-oo-eh lool]*	じじい *[jee-jee]*
S'envoyer en l'air *[senh-vooah-yair]*	**Platgaan** *[plaht-chkaahn]*	寝る *[neh-loo]*
Bouge de la *[boosh deh lah]*	**Rot op!** *[roht ohp]*	出ていけ *[deh-deh-ee-keh]*
Tu déconnes! *[tooh daih-cohnn]*	**Pleur op** *[plehr ohp]*	いいかげんにして *[ee-kah-gen-nee-shee-teh]*
Ministéréo portable *[meeh-neeh-ss-taih-raihoh port-taih-bleh]*	id.	でかラジ *[deh-kah-lah-jee]*
Bancroche *[bahn-crouh-ssh]*	**Manke** *[mahn-keh]*	身障 *[sheen-shoh]*

English	Spanish	German

Gism
[jih-zihm]
Sperm.

Lechada
[leh-chah-dah]

Wichse
[viek-zeh]

Glich
[glihch]
A problem.

Macana
[mah-kah-nah]

Pferdefuß
[fehr-deh-fooz]

Glitzy
[glit-zee]
Gaudy.

Vulgar
[vool-gahr]

Grell
[grehll]

Go down
[goh dowhn]
To perform fellatio
or cunnilingus.

Chuparla
[choo-pahr-lah]

**Auf die Knie
fallen**
*[owf dee knee fah-
len]*

Gofer
[goh-fehr]
An assistant.
Abbreviation for go
for this, go for
that..

Recadero
[reh-kah-deh-roh]

Hiwi
[hee-vee]

Gold-digger
[gohld-dihg-gehr]
A woman who
chooses a man for
his money.

Mantenida
[mah-teh-nee-dah]

Goldgräberin
[gold-gre-beh-reen]

Gonzo
[gahn-zoh]
Adventure
journalist.

Memo
[meh-moh]

Glücksritter
[glooks-reet-ah]

French	Dutch	Japanese
Le jus *[laih shoos]*	**Houtlijm** *[hah-oot-lime]*	エス *[eh-soo]*
Un trouble *[ahn troo-bleh]*	**Stront aan de knikker** *[ss-trohnt ahn deh k-neeh-kehr]*	問題 *[mohn-dai]*
Tape à l'oeil *[tahp ah loh-eh-eel]*	**Patjepeeërig** *[pat-tje-peh-ee- hreh]*	けばけばしい *[keh-bah-keh-bah- shee]*
Tailler une pipe à quelqu'un *[taih-iehr ihn peep-peh]*	**Zuigen** *[zah-oo-chkehn]*	休憩する *[kyoo-kay-soo-loo]*
Un larbin *[ahn lahr-bahn]*	**Knechtje** *[knechk-ee-eh]*	すけっと *[soo-keh-toh]*
Une croqueuse de diamants *[oon-naih croh- kaih-sse]*	**Society-hoer** *[soh-sah-ee-tee hoohr]*	マニ- ギャル *[mah-nee-gyah-loo]*
Journaliste d'aventures *[sjoor-nah-leest dah-van-toohr]*	**Avonturen- journalist** *[ah-vohn-too-rehn sjoor-nahl-eest]*	あっちこっちジャ- ナリスト *[ah-chee-koh-chee- jah-nah-lees-toh]*

English	Spanish	German

Goof
[goof]
To play a
practicaljoke on
someone.

Broma
[broh-mah]

Doofe Nuß
[doo-fe noos]

Goombah
[goom-bah]
Italian expression
for friend or
croney.

Compa
[kohm-pah]

Kumpel
[koom-pel]

Goon
[goon]
A criminal who
strongarms
someone.

Matón
[mah-tohn]

**Schwerer
Junge**
[shve-reh yoon-geh]

Goose
[gooss]
Pinch someone's
buttocks.

Animar
[a-nee-mahr]

**Jmdn. in den
Arsch Kneifen**
*[yeh-man-den in
den arsh kniy-fen]*

Grass
[grahss]
Marijuana.

Grifa
[gree-fah]

Gras
[grass]

Grease mon-key
[greess muhn-kee]
A mechanic.

Mecánico
[meh-kah-nee-koh]

Schmiermaxe
[shmeer-mak-seh]

Greasy spoon
[gree-ssee spoon]
Cheap restaurant.

Antro
[ahn-troh]

Curry Sau
[kur-ryh zow]

French	Dutch	Japanese
Un couillon *[ahn cooih-iohn]*	Kutgeintje *[kut-chkah-een-tje]*	間抜け *[mah-noo-keh]*
Mon gar *[mohn gahr]*	Maatje *[maah-tje]*	ダχ *[dah-chee]*
Un gorille *[ahn goh-rihl]*	Pistole- paultje *[pees-toe-le pahl-tje]*	暴力犯 *[boh-lyo-koo-hahn]*
Mettre la main au cul *[maiht-treh lah maihn oh cuhl]*	Billeknijpen *[bill-ehk-nah-eep-ehn]*	つねつね *[tsoo-neh-tsoo-neh]*
L'herbe *[laihr-beh]*	Stuff *[ss-tooph]*	はっぱ *[hah-pah]j*
Mecano *[meh-cah-noh]*	Techneut *[tech-neh-oot]*	機械工 *[kee-kah-yee-koh]*
Restaurant routier *[rehs-toh-raahn roo-tee-eh]*	Gore tent *[chkoh-reh tehnt]*	大衆食堂 *[tai-shoo-sho-koo-doh]*

English	Spanish	German
Green *[green]* Inexperienced.	**Novato, -a** *[noh-vah-toh, -tah]*	**Grüner** *[gree-nah]*
Gremlin *[grehm-lihn]* Mischief maker.	**Demonio** *[deh-moh-nee-oh]*	**Unruhestifter** *[oon-roo-en-shteef-tah]*
Grief *[greef]* Problems or backtalk.	**Lío** *[lee-oh]*	**Gram** *[grahm]*
Grind *[grynd]* Daily chores.	**Rutina** *[roo-tee-nah]*	**Tretmühle** *[tret-mueh-leh]*
Gringo *[green-goh]* Spanish expression for Americans.	**Gringo** *[green-goh]*	**Ami** *[ah-mee]*
Grody *[groh-dee]* Disgusting, i.e., Grody to the max.	**Asqueroso** *[ahss-keh-roh-soh]*	**Potthäßlich** *[pot-hess-leesh]*
Gross *[grohss]* Disgusting.	**Grosero, a** *[groh-seh-roh, -rah]*	**Ekelhaft** *[eh-kel-haft]*
Groupie *[groo-pee]* An obsessive fan, often women who follow rock stars.	**Fan** *[fahn]*	**Groupie** *[groo-pee]*

French	Dutch	Japanese
Novice *[noh-vees]*	**Groen** *[chkroohn]*	青二才 *[ah-oh-nee-sai]*
Un lutin de malheur *[ahn loo-tahnd mal-lairh]*	**Herrieschopper** *[heh-hrees-schkoh-pehr]*	グレムリン *[goo-leh-moo-leen]*
Des emmerdes *[daihs ahn maihrds]*	**Sores** *[soh-rehs]*	屁理屈 *[heh-lee-koo-tsoo]*
Métro-boulot-dodo *[mah-troh boo-loh doh-doh]*	**Beslommeringen** *[behs-lohm-meh-hreeng-ehn]*	雑用 *[zah-tsoo-yoh]*
Gringo *[green-goh]*	**Yankee** *[ee-aahn-kee]*	アメ公 *[ah-meh-koh]*
Déguelasse *[daih-gohl-ass]*	**Smerig** *[ss-meh-hrechk]*	いやな *[ee-yah-nah]*
Gerban *[gaihr-bahn]*	**Goor** *[chkohr]*	気持ち悪い *[kee-moh-chee-vah-loo-ee]*
Un groupie *[ahn groo-peeh]*	**Groupie** *[groo-pee]*	おっかけ *[oh-kah-keh]*

113

English	Spanish	German

Grunge
[gruhnj]
Dirty. A sloppy style of fashion. A form of rock music which combines aspects of heavy metal music with the rhythm and distortion of punk rock music.

Guarro
[gwah-rroh]

Grunge
[grunj]

Grunt work
[gruhnt wohrk]
A hard job that requires little intelligence.

Trabajo fastidioso
[trah-bah-kho fahss-tee-dee-oh-soh]

Maloche
[mah-loh-heh]

Gumshoe
[guhm-shoo]
Detective.

Detective
[dee-tehk-tee-veh]

Leisetreter
[lai-zeh-treh-tah]

Gunk
[guhnk]
Sticky, gooey substance.

Residuo cochambroso
[reh-see-doo-oh ko-chahm-broh-soh]

Schleim
[shlime]

Guzzle
[guhz-zuhl]
Drink quickly.

Tragon
[trah-gahr]

Saufen
[zow-fehn]

Gyp
[jihp]
To cheat..

Engañar, timar
[ehn-gah-nyahr, tee-mahr]

Verarschen
[fehr-arsh-en]

French	Dutch	Japanese
La mode grunge *[lah mauhd groonch]*	**Morsig** *[moohr-sechk]*	ヒッピ- *[hee-pee]*
Un boulot à la con *[ahn boo-loh ah lah cohn]*	**Klotebaan** *[kloh-oo-teh-baahn]*	土方 *[doh-kah-tah]*
Condé *[cohn-daih]*	**Speurneus** *[ss-pehr-neh-oosh]*	探偵 *[tahn-tay]*
La pègue *[lah paihg]*	**Kleverige troep** *[kleh-ee-veh-reh-chkeh t-hroop]*	ねばっこい *[neh-bah-koy]*
Lever le coud *[leh-vehl coohd]*	**Naar achteren klokken** *[naahr achk-teh-hrehn klok-kehn]*	早飲み *[hah-yah-no-mee]*
Estamper *[eh-tahm-paihr]*	**Besodemieteren** *[beh-soh-deh-mee-teh-hrehn]*	ぺてんにかける *[peh-tehn-nee-kah-keh-loo]*

English	Spanish	German
Gypsy cab	**Taxi**	**Schwarztaxi**
[jihp-see kahb]	*[tahkss-ee]*	*[shvarts-tak-see]*
An independent taxi driver .		

French	Dutch	Japanese
Taxi indepen-dent *[tak-see ahn-deh-pahn-dahn]*	**Snorder** *[ss-noh-rdehr]*	しろタク *[shee-loh-tah-koo]*

H

is for...

Hooker

English	Spanish	German
Hack [hahk] Cab driver.	**Taxista** [tahkss-eess-tah]	**Kutscher** [koot-shah]
Hairy [hayr-ree] A situation fraught with danger or difficulties.	**Peludo, -a** [peh-loo-doh, -dah]	**Haarige Situation** [har-ree-geh sit-u-ah-tsee-yon]
Half-assed [hahf-ahsst] To do something without enthusiasm.	**Hacer sin ganas** [ah-thehr seen gah-nahss]	**Halbherzig** [hahlb-herr-tseeg]
Ham [hahm] Someone who craves the lime-light.	**Divo, -a** [dee-voh, -vah]	**Mediengeiler Kerl** [me-dien-guy-lah kerl]
Hand-job [hahnd-johb] To assist a man to masturbate.	**Masturbar a alguien** [mah-stuhr-bahr ah ahl-kee-ehn]	**Partnerwix** [part-nah veeks]
Hanky panky [hahn-kee pahn-kee] Sex play.	**Manosearse** [mah-noh-seh-ahrr-seh]	**Sexspiel** [sex-shpeel]
Hard ass [hahrd-ahss] A person who insists on the rules	**Estricto, -a** [ehss-treek-toh, -tah]	**Hartstühler** [hart-shtoo-lah]

French	Dutch	Japanese
Un chauffeur *[ahn shohf-fehr]*	**Taxichauffeur** *[tax-ee shoh-fehr]*	運ちゃん *[oon-chahn]*
Epineux *[eh-peen-eh]*	**Linke soep** *[leen-keh soop]*	難儀 *[nahn-gee]*
Malfait *[mahl-feht]*	**Halfzacht** *[half-zachkt]*	半端 *[hahn-pah]*
Un poseur *[ahn poh-sehr]*	**Publiciteitsgeil** *[poo-blee-see-tah-eet-ss-chkehl]*	大根役者 *[dai-kohn-yah-koo-shah]*
Branler quelqu'un *[brahn-leh kail-kan]*	**Iemamd aftrekken** *[ee-mahnd ahf-t-hrehk-kehn]*	しごく *[shee-go-koo]*
Un coup fourré *[ahn koop foo-raih]*	**Sexen** *[seks-ehn]*	セックス *[seh-koo-soo]*
Un dur *[ahn doohr]*	**Ambtenaar** *[amb-teh-naahr]*	堅い人 *[kah-shee-koh-yee-hee-toh]*

English	Spanish	German
Hardball *[hahrd-bahl]* Serious busines.	**En serio** *[ehn seh-ree-oh]*	**Seriöse Transaktion** *[zeh-ree-o-zeh trans-akt-zee-yon]*
Hard-on *[hahrd-ohn]* An erection.	**Empalmado, trempado** *[ehm-pahl-mah-do, trehm-pah-do]*	**Einen Harten haben** *[aiy-nen har-ten hah-ben]*
Hatchet job *[hahch-eht johb]* To disparage someone.	**Maltratar, chapuza** *[mahl-trah-tahr, chah-poo-tha]*	**Jmdn.verächt-lich machen** *[yeh-man-den fer-esht-leesh mah-hen]*
Heater *[hee-tehr]* A gun.	**Pistola, pipa** *[pee-stoh-lah, pee-pah]*	**Kanone** *[kah-no-neh]*
Heave-ho *[heev-hoh]* Get rid of someone.	**Deshacerse de alguien** *[deh-sah-thehn-seh deh ahl-gee-ehn]*	**Zu jmd.den Rücken kehren** *[tsoo yeh-man-den den rik-ken ker-ren]*
Heavy *[heh-vee]* Bad guy.	**Pesado** *[peh-sah-doh]*	**Schwerer Junge** *[shveh-reh yoon-geh]*
Heinie *[hy-nee]* Buttocks.	**Nalgas** *[nahl-gahss]*	**Arsch** *[arsh]*

French	Dutch	Japanese
C'est du sérieux! *[seh doo saih-rieh]*	Om 't echie *[ohm-eht-echk-ee]*	大仕事 *[oh-shee-go-toh]*
Bander *[bahn-deh]*	Paal *[paahl]*	堅くなる *[kah-shee-ko-koo-nah-roo]*
Démonter quelqu'un ou quelque chose *[deh-mohn-taih kehl-kahn]*	Iemand zwart maken *[ee-mahnd z-vahrt maah-kehn]*	けなす *[keh-nah-soo]*
Un pétard *[ahn peh-tahr]*	Een blaffer *[ehn blahf-fehr]*	ピストル *[pee-soo-toh-loo]*
Plaquer quelqu'un *[plah-keh kehl-ahn]*	Iemand dumpen *[ee-mahnd dehm-pehn]*	消す *[keh-soo]*
Un vicieux *[ahn vee-see-eh]*	Boef *[boohf]*	悪い奴 *[wah-loo-ee-yah-tsoo]*
Le postère *[leh pohs-tehre]*	Kont *[kohnt]*	尻 *[shee-lee]*

English	Spanish	German

Hell
[hehl]
Mild expression of distaste or frustration.

¡Mierda!
[mee-ehrr-dah]

Hölle
[hoo-leh]

Hellacious
[hchl ay shihss]
Awful.

Genial
[gheh-nee-ahl]

Höllisch
[hoo-lish]

Hick
[hihk]
A country bumpkin.

Campesino, -a
[kahm-peh-see-noh]

Trampel
[tram-pel]

Hickey
[hihkee]
A red mark (usually on the neck or breasts) from a strenuous kiss.

Morete
[moh-reh-teh]

Knutschfleck
[knootsh-flehk]

High
[hy]
The effect of various drugs.

Vuelo
[voo-eh-loh]

High
[hlgh]

Hip
[hihp]
Cool. In the know.

De moda
[deh moh-dah]

Hip
[hip]

Hit man
[hiht mahn]
An assassin.

Asesino, maton
[ah-seh-see-no, mah-tohn]

Mörder
[mur-dah]

French	Dutch	Japanese
Ras le bol! *[rhahs leh bohl]*	**Getsie** *[chket-see-eh]*	地獄 *[jee-go-koo]*
Inférnal *[ahn-fehr-nahl]*	**Klote** *[kloh-oo-teh]*	地獄のような *[jee-go-koo-no-yo-nah]*
Rustaud *[ahn rhus-tohd]*	**Boerelul** *[boo-reh-leh-ool]*	イモ *[ee-moh]*
Un suçon *[ahn soos-sohn]*	**Zuigzoen** *[zaa-oochk-zoohn]*	キスマーク *[kee-soo-mah-koo]*
être parti(e) *[ehtr pahr-tee]*	**High** *[hy]*	ハイ *[high]*
Branché *[brahn-shai]*	**Hip** *[hip]*	きれる *[kee-leh-loo]*
Assassin *[ahs-sah-sahn]*	**Huurmoorde-naar** *[hoohr-mohr-deh-nahr]*	殺し屋 *[ko-lo-shee-yah]*

English	Spanish	German

Hock
[hahk]
To put a possession in a pawn shop. In debt.

Empeñar
[ehm-peh-nyahr]

Verpfänden
[fehr-fen-den]

Ho
[hoh]
Black slang for a "whore" or prostitute. Degrogatory for woman.

Puta
[poo-tah]

Schlampe
[shlam-peh]

Hoisted by his own petard
[hoy-stehd by hihz ohn pih-tahrd]
To put your foot in your mouth. Get in trouble through your own efforts.

Se colgó
[seh kohl-goh]

Jmd. steht sich selbst im Weg
[yeh-mand shtayt zeesh zelbst eem veg]

Homeboy
[hohm-boy]
Black slang for someome local or a friend.

Compadre
[kohm-pah-dreh]

Laheim
[la-haim]

Honkers
[hahn-kehrz]
Breasts.

Tetas
[teh-tahss]

Memmen
[mem-men]

Hooch
[hooch]
Cheap alcohol.

Ron de quemar
[rohn deh keh-mahr]

Sprit
[shpreet]

French	Dutch	Japanese
En gage *[ahn gash]*	**Naar Ome Jan brengen** *[naahr ohmeh yann bhrehn-gehn]*	質に入れる *[shee-tsoo-nee-ee-reh-loo]*
Une radasse *[oon-eh rhah-dahs-eh]*	**Hoerekoppie** *[hoo-eh-reh-kop-pee]*	売女 *[bai-tah]*
Se foutre dedans *[seh foohtr deh-danse]*	**Jezelf in de voet schieten** *[ee-ehs-self ihn deh vooht ss-chkeet-tehn]*	自業自得 *[jee-goh-jee-toh-koo]*
Homeboy *[ohm-boh-ee]*	**Maatje** *[maah-tje]*	ダχ *[dah-chee]*
Des nénés *[deh neh-neh]*	**Peren** *[pee-eh-rehn]*	乳 *[chee-chee]*
Gnôle *[nohl]*	**Spiritus** *[ss-pee-reeh-toos]*	安酒 *[yah-soo-zah-keh]*

English	Spanish	German
Hooker [huh-kehr] A prostitute.	**Put** [poo-tah]	**Nutte** [noo-teh]
Hoot [hoot] Something funny. A laugh.	**Payasada** [pah-yah-sah-dah]	**Gejohle** [geh-yo-leh]
Hooters [hoot-ehrz] Breasts.	**Tetas** [teh-tahss]	**Milch Gebirge** [meelsh geh-beer-geh]
Horny [hohr-nee] Sexually aroused.	**Cachondo, -a ; arrecho, -a** [kah-chohn-doh, -dah ah-rreh-choh, -chah]	**Geil** [guyl]
Hot [haht] Sexually aroused.	**Cachondo, -a; caliente** [kah-chohn-doh, kah-lee-ehn-teh]	**Aufgeheizt** [auf-geh-haits]
How's it hangin? [hous eet hangeen] How are you?	**¿Qué tal?** [keh tahl]	**Wie geht's, wie steht's?** [vee gayts, vee shtayts]

French	Dutch	Japanese
Une raccrocheuse *[oon-eh rhac-croh-shehse]*	Hoertje *[hoo-ee-rtje]*	売春婦 *[bai-shoon-hoo]*
C'est tordant *[seh tohr-dahn]*	Dijenkletser *[dah-ee-ehn-klet-tsehr]*	お笑い *[oh-wah-lah-ee]*
Des boudonnes *[deh booh-dohn-neh]*	Bloemkolen *[bloom-kolen]*	むね *[moo-neh]*
Avoir la canne *[ah-vooar lah cahn]*	Hitsig *[heet-sechk]*	エロい *[eh-lo-ee]*
Avoir le feu aux fesses *[ah-vuahr leh feh oh fehs]*	Gruizig *[chkrah-oo-zichk]*	いやらしい *[ee-yah-lah-shee]*
La peche *[lah peh-sh]*	De koffer induiken met *[deh kohf-fehr een-dah-oo-kehn met]*	どう? *[doh]*

English	Spanish	German

Hump
[huhmp]
To have sex with.

Follar
[foh-yahr]

Bohnern
[boh-nehn]

Hustler
[huhss-lehr]
Someone who takes
advantage of
others.

Abusón
[ah-boo-sohn]

Trittbrettfahrer
[trit-bret-far-rah]

Hype
[hyp]
Create excitment
about something.

Fiebre
[fee-eh-breh]

Echauffieren
[eh-shau-fear-ren]

French	Dutch	Japanese
Faire une partie de jambes en l'air *[fehr oon-eh pahr-teeh deh shamb ahn lehr]*	**Uitvreter** *[ah-oot-vreh-ee-tehr]*	やる *[yah-loo]*
Un brasseur *[ahn brhas-sher]*	**Rage** *[hrah-sje]*	ズル *[zoo-loo]*
Un gros coup de pub *[ahn grohss koopd pob]*	**Omleggen** *[ohm-lechkehn]*	盛り上げる *[moh-lee-ah-geh-loo]*

I

is for...
Icky

English	Spanish	German

Ice
[eiss]
To kill.

Eliminar
[eh-lee-mee-nahr]

Kaltmachen
[kult-mah-chen]

Icky
[ih-kee]
Cloying or senti-mental.

Sentimental
[sehn-tee-mehn-tahl]

Sentimental
[zehn-tee-mehn-tahl]

Iffy
[ih-fee]
Not definite.

Indeciso
[een-deh-thee-soh]

Lauwarm
[lau-varm]

Inside job
[ihn-ssyd johb]
To be robbed by someone whom you know.

Fraude, pufo
[frah-oo-deh, poo-foh]

Vom besten Freund ausgenommen werden
[fome bes-ten freund aus-gen-o-men ver-den]

Item
[it-ehm]
Two people having a romance.

Pareja
[pah-reh-khah]

Eine Affäre haben
[aiy-neh af-feh-reh hah-ben]

French	Dutch	Japanese
Refroidir quelqu'un *[reh-fruah-dirh kehl-kahn]*	**Zoetsappig** *[zoot-sap-pechk]*	やる *[yah-loo]*
De la guimauve *[deh lah geeh-mohv-eh]*	**Onzeker** *[ohn-zeh-ee-kehr]*	おセンχ *[oh-sehn-chee]*
Douteux *[dooh-teh]*	**Matenaaier** *[mah-tehn-ah-ee-ehr]*	あやふやな *[ah-yah-hoo-yah-nah]*
Un coup monté *[ahn koop-mohn-taih]*	**Tortelduifjes** *[tohr-tehl-dah-oo-fjes]*	内輪泥棒 *[oo-chi-wah-doh-loh-boh]*
Une affaire *[oon-eh ah-fehr]*	**Oetlul** *[oot-leh-ool]*	できてる *[deh-kee-teh-loo]*

J

is for...

Jumper

English	Spanish	German

Jackass
[jahk-ahss]
Someone stupid.

Burro, -a
[boo-rroh,-rrah]

Simpel
[zim-pehl]

Jag
[jahg]
A destructive spree
involving drinking,
drugs or crying.

Pasota
[pah-soh-tah]a

Sauftour
[zauf-taur]

Jail bait
[jayl-bayt]
A sexy underage
girl or boy.

Yogurcito, a
[yoh-guhr-thee-toh, -tah]

Jugendliches Gift
[yu-gen-dleeshes gift]

JAP
[jahp]
Jewish American
Princess (spoiled
girl). Derogatory
word for Japanese.

Japonés
[kha-poh-nehss]

Japs
[yaps]

Jerk
[jehrk]
*Someone selfish,
mean or repellant
for any number of
reasons.*

Repelente
[reh-peh-lehn-teh]

Kotzbrocken
[kots-bro-ken]

Jerk-off
[jehrk-ohff]
Masturbate.

Pajearse
[pah-kheh-ahr-seh]

Hol dir einen runter
[hole dir ai-nen run-tah]

Jock
[jahk]
An atheIete.

Atleta
[aht-leh-tah]

Kraftmensch
[kraft-mensh]

French	Dutch	Japanese
Un couillon *[ahn cooh-ee-ion]*	**Bralpartij** *[brahl-pahr-tah-ee]*	たわけ *[tah-wah-keh]*
Faire la bombe *[fehr lah bohmb]*	**Knaapje** *[k-nah-pee-ee-eh]*	馬鹿騒ぎ *[bah-kah-sah-wah-gee]*
Un faux poids *[ahn foh pooah]*	**Spleetoog** *[ss-pleh-ee-tochk]*	ませガキ *[mah-seh-gah-kee]*
Jap *[shap]*	**Jap** *[yahp]*	日本人 *[nee-hohn-jeen]*
Un con *[ahn kohn]*	**Trekken** *[threhk-kehn]*	いやな奴 *[ee-yah-nah-yah-tsoo]*
Se branler *[seh brahn-leh]*	**Klerekast** *[klee-eh-reh-kast]*	一人遊び *[hee-toh-ree-ah-so-bee]*
Un fana de sport *[ahn fah-nah dehs-pohrt]*	**Tok** *[tohk]*	競技者 *[kyo-gee-shah]*

139

English	Spanish	German
Jock strap *[jahk sstrahp]* Protective device for male genitalia worn for sports.	**Suspensor** *[soo-spehn-sohr]*	**Sackschützer** *[zak-shoo-tzer]*
John *[jahn]* Bathroom.	**Water** *[vah-tehr]*	**Naßzelle** *[nas-tsel-leh]*
Joint *[joynt]* A marijuana cigarette.	**Porro ; pito** *[poh-rroh, pee-toh]*	**Joint** *[johint]*
Jugs *[juhgz]* Breasts.	**Tetas** *[teh-tahss]*	**Milchkannen** *[milsh-kan-nen]*
Juice *[jooss]* Alcohol.	**Combustible, caldo** *[kohm-booss-tee- bleh, kahl-doh]*	**Wässerle** *[ve-ser-leh]*
Jumper *[juhm-pehr]* Someone who commits suicide by leaping off a high place.	**Suicida** *[soo-ee-thee-dah]*	**Springer** *[spring-ah]*
Jump your bones *[juhmp yohr bohnz]* Have sexual intercourse.	**Follar** *[foh-yahr]*	**Jmdn. aufs Kreuz legen** *[yeh-man-den aufs kreuz leh-gen]*

French	Dutch	Japanese
Un soutien-couilles *[ahn sooh-tiahn-koo-ih-eh]*	**Zak beschermer** *[zahk bee-shehr-mehr]*	サポ-タ- *[sah-poh-tah]*
Les chiottes *[leh shee-oht]*	**Plee** *[play]*	便所 *[ben-jo]*
Un joint *[ahn shooan]*	**Joint** *[jo-eent]*	ジョイント *[jo-een-toh]*
Des rotoplots *[deh roh-toh-ploh]*	**Memmen** *[meh-mehn]*	おっぱい *[oh-pai]*
Gnôle *[niolh]*	**Neut** *[neh-oot]*	おちゃけ *[oh-chah-keh]*
Un suicide *[ahn soo-ih-seed]*	**Springer** *[ss-preen-hgehr]*	飛び降り *[toh-bee-oh-ree]*
voir "HUMP"	**Rampetampen** *[hrahm-peh-tahm-pehn]*	寝る *[neh-loo]*

English	Spanish	German
Junk *[juhnk]* Heroin.	**Heroína, caballo** *[eh-roh-ee-nah, kah-bah-yoh]*	**Eidsch** *[aych]*
Junkie *[juhn-kee]* Drug addict person.	**Yonki** *[yohn-kee]*	**Junkie** *[juhn-kee]*

French	Dutch	Japanese
La poudre *[lah poohdr]*	id.	ペ *[peh]*
Drogué *[drhoh-geh]*	id.	ヤク中 *[yah-koo-choo]*

K

is for...
Kinky

English	Spanish	German

Kaput
[kah-puht]
Finished, destroyed.

¡Kaput!
[kah-poot]

Kaputt
[kah-poot]

Kibosh
[kee-bohsh]
Put an end to
something.

Ponerle fin
[poh-nehr-leh feen]

Abkacken
[ab-kah-ken]

Kick
[kihk]
Fun. Exciting
experience.

Diversión
[dee-vehr-see-ohn]

Kick
[kihk]

**Kick the
bucket**
*[kihk thah buhk-
eht]*
To die.

Palmarla
[pah-mahr-lah]

**Den Löffel
abgeben**
*[den loo-fel ab-geh-
ben]*

Kinky
[keen-kee]
Something sexually
unusual.

Pervertido
[pehr-vehr-tee-doh]

Abartig
[ab-ar-tij]

Kip
[kihp]
A dive, usally refers
to a bar or a cheap
hotel.

**Sitio de mala
muerte**
*[see-tee-oh deh
mah-lah mwehr-
teh]*

Spelunke
[speh-loon-keh]

Kishkes
[kihsh-kuhss]
Guts. (Yiddish
slang)

Tener cojones
*[teh-nehr ko-kho-
nehss]*

Gedärm
[geh-derm]

French	Dutch	Japanese
Cassé *[kah-seh]*	Naar de haaien *[naahr deh haa-ee-ehn]*	おわり *[oh-wah-ree]*
Mettre le hola à quelqu'un *[mehtr loh-lah ah kelk-kahn]*	Kappen *[kah-pehn]* id.	とどめをさす *[toh-doh-meh-oh-sah-soo]*
Un frisson de plaisir *[ahn frhee-sohnd pleh-seehr]*	Kassie zes *[kah-see zehs]*	刺激 *[shee-geh-kee]*
Casser sa pipe *[kaah-seh sah peep]*	id.	おだ仏 *[oh-dah-boo-tsoo]*
Eccentrique *[x-ehn-trhick]*	Tent *[tehnt]*	変タイ *[hen-tah-yee]*
Un boui-boui *[ahn boo-ih booh-ih]*	Kishkes *[kish-kehs]*	酒場 *[sah-kah-bah]*
Boyaux *[bo-eeh-oh]*	Slome *[ss-loh-oo-meh]*	ガッツ *[gah-tsoo]*

English	Spanish	German

Klutz
[kluhtz]
Someone clumsey.

Torpe, patoso
[tohr-peh, pah-toh-soh]

Trampel
[tram-pel]

Knocked-up
[nahkt-uhp]
Make pregnant.

Preñar
[preh-nyahrr]

Eine Frau aufpumpen
[ai-neh frow auf-poom-pen]

Knock-off
[nahk-ohff]
To finish work, kill someone or make a copy of something for sale (i.e., a Chanel bag for $10).

Terminar con
[tehr-mee-mahr kohn]

Schlußmachen
[shloos-mah-chen]

Knockers
[nah-kehrz]
Breasts.

Pechugas
[peh-choo-gahss]

Vorbau
[fohr-bow]

Kosher
[koh-shehr]
Correct or legal.

Legal
[leh-gahl]

Koscher
[ko-sher]

Kraut
[krowht]
Derogatory for German.

Cabeza cuadrada
[cah-beh-thah kwa-drah-dah]

Piefke
[peef-keh]

Kvetch
[kvehch]
Whine or complain.

Quejarse
[keh-kharh-seh]

Jaulen
[yow-len]

French	Dutch	Japanese
Andouille *[ahn-doo-eeh-ieh]*	**Dekken** *[dehk-kehn]*	ドジ *[doh-jee]*
Avoir un pouchinelle dans le tiroir *[ah-vooh-ahr ahn polee-shee-nehl dahnl tee-roo-ahr]*	**Ermee kappen** *[ehr-meh-ee kohp-pehn]*	はらませる *[hah-lah-mah-seh-loo]*
S'en filér *[sahn fee-lehr]*	**Meloenen** *[meh-loo-nehn]*	片付ける *[kah-tah-zoo-keh-loo]*
voir "HONKERS"	**id.**	ぼいん *[boy-yeen]*
Réglo *[reh-gloh]*	**Mof** *[mohf]*	生 *[nah-mah]*
Fritz *[freets]*	**Zeuren** *[zeh-eh-hrehn]*	ドイツ人 *[doh-yee-tsoo-jeen]*
Geignard *[gah-niarhd]*	**Stompzinnig** *[ss-toomp-zin-echk]*	ぶつぶつ言う *[boo-tsoo-boo-tsoo-yoo]*

L

is for...

Lardass

English	Spanish	German

Lame
[laym]
Stupid.

Idiota
[idiota]

Unterbelichtet
[oon-ter-beh-leesh-tet]

Lard ass
[lahrd-ahss]
Fat, slow, lazy person.

Pisa huevos
[pee-sah weh-bohss]

Stinkfaul
[stink-foul]

Lark
[lahrk]
For fun.

Divertido, -a
[dee-vehr-tee-doh, -dah]

Aus Jux
[ows yooks]

Leak
[leek]
To urinate.

Chorrear
[choh-rreh-ahr]

Pullern
[poo-lehn]

Lech
[lehch]
Abbreviation for lecher: dirty old man.

Viejo verde
[vee-eh-kho behr-deh]

Lüstling
[loost-ling]

Lemon
[leh-mohn]
A poor specimen, usually a car.

Carcocha
[kahr-koh-chah]

Zitrone
[tsee-tro-neh]

Liquid lunch
[lih-kwihd luhnch]
A meal without the food.

Borrachera
[bow-rrah-cheh-rah]

Flüssiges Mittagessen
[floo-see-ges mit-tak-es-sen]

Loaded
[loh-dehd]
Drunk or high on drugs.

Colocado
[kow-low-kah-doh]

Besoffen
[beh-zo-fen]

French	Dutch	Japanese
Abruti *[ah-broo-tee]*	**Vet varken** *[veht vahrk-kehn]*	のうたりん *[noh-tah-reen]*
Gros tas *[groh tah]*	**Voor de lol** *[voohr deh lohl]*	のろま *[no-lo-mah]*
Une franci *[oon-eh frahn-see]*	**Pissen** *[pis-sehn]*	ジョ-クで *[jo-koo-deh]*
égoutter la sardine *[eh-goo-tehr lah sahr-deen]*	**Ouwe viezerik** *[ah-oo-eh vee-zeh-reek]*	しょんべんする *[shohn-ben-soo-loo]*
Un cavaleur *[ahn cah-vah-lehr]*	**Barrel** *[bah-hrohl]*	じいさん *[jee-sahn]*
Un mauvais numéro *[ahn moh-veh noo-meh-roh]*	**Vloiebaar twaalfuurtje** *[vloo-ee-bahr tvahlf-uhurtje]*	おんぼろ *[ohn-boh-loh]*
Une beuverie *[oon-eh beh-veh-ree]*	**In de lorem** *[ihn deh loh-rehm]*	大酒のみ *[oh-zah-keh-no-me]*
Bourré *[booh-rheh]*	**Luie donder** *[lah-oo-ee-eh dohn-dehr]*	酔っ払った *[yo-pah-lah-tah]*

English	Spanish	German
Loafer *[loh-fehr]* Someone who hangs around; lazy.	**Perezoso** *[peh-reh-tho-so]*	**Faulenzer** *[foul-len-tsah]*
Loco *[loh-koh]* Crazy.	**Loco** *[low-kow]*	**Spinner** *[shpee-nah]*
Loo *[loo]* Bathroom.	**Baño** *[bah-nyow]*	**Topf** *[topf]*
Looker *[luh-kehr]* Attractive woman.	**Preciosa** *[preh-cee-oh-sah]*	**Augenweide** *[ow-gen-vai-deh]*
Loony bin *[loo-nee bihn]* Mental institution.	**Manicomio** *[mah-nee-kow-mee-oh]*	**Klapse** *[klap-seh]*
Looped *[loopt]* Drunk or stoned.	**Dopado** *[dow-pah-dow]*	**Im Tran sein** *[ihm trahn zahin]*
Loot *[loot]* Money.	**Lana** *[lah-nah]*	**Beute** *[boi-teh]*
Lush *[luhsh]* An alcoholic person.	**Borracho** *[bow-rrah-chow]*	**Schluckspecht** *[shlook-shpesht]*

French	Dutch	Japanese
Un glandeur *[ahn glahn-dehr]*		のらくら者 *[no-lah-koo-lah-mo-no]*
Dingo *[den-goh]*	**Gestoord** *[chkehs-tohrt]*	気違い *[kee-chee-guy]*
Chiot *[shee-oht]*	**Plee** *[play]*	便所 *[ben-jo]*
Un joli lot *[ahn sho-lee loh]*	**Mokkeltje** *[moh-kohl-tje]*	生かす女 *[ee-kah-soo-ohn-nah]*
Asile de dingues *[ah-seeld dahng]*	**Gekkenhuis** *[chkeh-kehn-hauss]*	精神病院 *[say-sheen-byo-een]*
Rond *[rhon]*	**In de olie** *[ihn deh o-lee]*	酔った *[yo-tah]*
Pognon *[poh-nion]*	**Buit** *[bah-oot]*	かね *[kah-neh]*
Soulard(e) *[soo-lahrd]*	**Drankorgel** *[dhrahnk-ohr-chkohl]*	アル中 *[ah-loo-choo]*

M

is for...

Made

157

English	Spanish	German
Made [mayd] A member of the mafia.	**Mafioso** [mah-fee-oh-soh]	**Mafioso** [ma-fee-o-zoh]
Main-line [mayn-lyn] Inject heroin.	**Inyectarse** [in-yek-tar-seh]	**Drücken** [dree-ken]
Make [mayk] Have sexual intercourse.	**Acostarse con alguien** [ah-ko-star-se con al-gee-en]	**Eine Nummer schieben** [ai-neh noo-mah shee-ben]
Mark [mahrk] Person who attracts a criminal assult.	**Vícitma** [vik-ti-ma]	**Eine bedeutende Kriminelle Persönlichkeit** [ai-neh beh-doi-ten-deh kree-mee-neh-leh per-zohn-lish-kite]
Meat [meet] Penis.	**Miembro** [mee-em-broh]	**Latte** [lat-teh]
Meat-market [meet-mahr-keht] Singles bar.	**Bar de solterones** [bar de sol-tay-roh-nes]	**Fleischbeschau** [flysh-beh-shao]
Mensch [mehnsh] A good, honest man.	**Buena gente** [bwena hen-tay]	**Ein Mensch** [ain mensh]

French	Dutch	Japanese
Un mafioso *[ahn mah-fee-oh-soh]*	**Mafioos** *[mah-fee-oh-oos]*	やあさん *[yah-sahn]*
Se shooter *[seh shoo-teh]*	**Spuiten** *[ss-pah-oo-tehn]*	ヤクをうつ *[yah-koo-oh-oo-tsoo]*
Lever une femme *[leh-veh oohn-eh fahm]*	**Wippen** *[vip-pehn]*	寝る *[neh-loo]*
Pigeon *[pee-shohn]*	**Je vraagt erom** *[ee-eh vraachkt ehr-ohm]*	常習犯 *[jo-shoo-hahn]*
La bite *[lah biht]*	**Boompie** *[boh-oom-pee]*	ダイコン *[dai-kohn]*
Un bar pour dragueurs *[ahn bahr poohr drah-gehr]*	**Vleesmarkt** *[vleh-ees-markt]*	シングルバ- *[seen-goo-loo-bah]*
Un mec réglo *[ahn mehk rheh-gloh]*	**Brave borst** *[bhrah-veh bohrscht]*	まじめ男 *[mah-jee-meh-oh-toh-koh]*

English	Spanish	German

Mick
[mihk]
Derogatory for
Irish.

Irlandés
[ir-lan-des]

Irisch
[ear-ish]

Mickey mouse
[mih-kee mowhss]
Easy. Often used to
describe a college
course like physical
education.

Fácil
[fah-thil]

Baby-einfach
[bay-bee-ain-fuch]

M.O.
[ehm-oh]
Used to describe a
criminalís pattern
(Abbreviation for
modus
operandus).
Typical behavior.

**Modus
operandi**
[mo-dus oh-per-an-dee]

Raster
[ras-tah]

Mob
[mahb]
The Mafia.

Mafia
[mah-fee-ah]

Mafia
[mah-fee-ah]

**Monday
morning
quarterback**
[muhn-day mohr-neen kwahr-tehr bahk]
Someone who
indulges in
hindsight.

Lamento
[lah-men-tow]

Hinterlader
[hin-ter-la-dah]

Murphy's law
[muhr-feez lawh]
Whatever can go
wrong will..

**Lo que es
mierda,mierda
sera**
[low kay es mee-er-dah,mee-er-dah seh--rah]

Pechströhne
[pesh-strooh-neh]

French	Dutch	Japanese
Une pomme de terre *[oon-eh pohmd tehr]*	**Eitje** *[eye-tee-eh]*	アイルランド人 *[ah-yee-loo-lahn-doh-jeen]*
Fastoche *[phas-tosh]*	**m.o.**	ちょろい *[jo-lo-yee]*
Louche *[loosh]*		手口 *[teh-goo-chee]*
Le mafia *[leh mah-fee-ah]*	**Mafia** *[mah-fee-ah]*	ちんぴら *[cheen-pee-lah]*
"Si j'avais su" *[see shaveh sooh]*	**Betweter** *[bet-veh-ee-tehr]*	知ったかぶり *[shee-tah-kah-boo-ree]*
Pessimisme *[peh-see-meesm-eh]*	**De wet van Murphy** *[deh veht vohn Muhr-fee]*	マ-フィ-の法則 *[mah-fee-no-ho-so-koo]*

English	Spanish	German
Monkey suit *[muhn-kee soot]* A Tuxedo.	**Traje de pingüino** *[trah-hay de peen-gwee-noh]*	**Smoking** *[smo-king]*
Moocher *[moo-chehr]* Someone who tries to live off peopleís generosity.	**Aprovechado** *[ah-proh-beh-chah-doh]*	**Schmarotzer** *[shma-ro-tzah]*
Moon *[moon]* Reveal your buttocks to someone as a joke. Commonly done by teenagers in cars.	**Enseñar el culo** *[en-se-nyar el koo-low]*	**Arschgesicht** *[arsh-geh-zeesht]*
Moonlight *[moon-lyt]* Work a second job.	**Trabajo alternativo** *[trah-bah-hoh al-ter-nah-tee-voh]*	**Zweitberuf** *[tsvait-beh-roof]*
Mother fucker *[muh-thehr fuh-kehr]* A contemptible person.	**Hijo de puta** *[ee-ho de poo-ta]*	**Paria** *[par-ree-ah]*
Mouthpiece *[mowhth-peess]* Someone who speaks for someone else, i.e., a lawyer or publicist .	**Representante** *[reh-preh-sen-tan-tay]*	**Sprachrohr** *[shprach-rohr]*

French	Dutch	Japanese
Le smok' *[leh smohk]*	**Apepakkie** *[ah-peh-pah-kee]*	タキシ-ド *[tah-kee-shee-doh]*
Glandeur *[glahn-dehr]*	**Parasiet** *[ph-hrah-seet]*	乞食 *[ko-jee-kee]*
Faire voir la lune en plein jour *[fehr voo-ahr lah loohn ahn plehn shoohr]*	**Moonen** *[moh-oo-nehn]*	尻を見せる *[shee-ree-oh-mee-seh-loo]*
Travailler au noir *[trah-vaih-ehr oh nooh-ahr]*	**D'r bijklussen** *[dehr by-kloos-ehn]*	夜番 *[yah-bahn]*
Enculé de sa mère *[ahn-cool-ehd sah mehr]*	**Hondekop** *[hohn-deh-kohp]*	げす野郎 *[geh-soo-yah-loh]*
Une porte-parole *[oon-eh pohrt-parohl]*	**Spreekbuis** *[ss-preheek-bah-ush]*	代弁者 *[dai-ben-shah]*

English	Spanish	German

Mucho
[moo-choh]
A lot.

Mucho
[moo-choh]

Ein ganzes Stall voll...
[ain gan-tzes shtal foll]

Muff
[muhf]
A woman's genitals.

Coño
[ko-nyoh]

Fut
[foot]

Muff diver
[muhf-dy-vehr]
Perform cunnilingus.

Cunnilingus
[cun-nee-lin-gus]

Fotzelecker
[foh-tzeh-leh-kah]

Mug shot
[muhg-shaht]
Picture of someone (From police photograph).

Retrato policial
[reh-trah-toh po-lee-thial]

Verbrecheral-benfoto
[fehr-breh-sher-al-ben-fo-toh]

Mule
[myool]
Someone who transports drugs usually inside their body.

Camello
[kah-may-yo]

Maultier
[mowl-tear]

Munchies
[muhn-cheez]
A hungry feeling as a result of smoking marijuana.

Jala
[chah-lah]

Freßlust
[fres-loost]

French	Dutch	Japanese
Trop *[troh]*	**Zooitje** *[zoh-ee-tje]*	一杯 *[ee-pie]*
La chatte *[lah shaht]*	**Oerwoud** *[oo-ehr-vah-oot]*	繁み *[shee-geh-mee]*
Un lécheur de minette *[ahn leh-shehrd meen-neht]*	**Beffer** *[beh-fehr]*	繁み探索 *[shee-geh-mee-tahn-sah-koo]*
Le trombinoscope *[leh trohm-bee-nos-cohp]*	**Fotootje** *[fo-ooh-toh-tje]*	人相写真 *[neen-soh-shah-sheen]*
Un passeur *[ahn pahs-sehr]*	**Koerier** *[koo-ree-ee-ehr]*	ワタリ *[wah-tah-ree]*
Avoir la dalle *[ah-voo-ahr lah dahl]*	**Vreetkick** *[vreh-eet-kick]*	渇望感 *[kah-tsoo-boh-kahn]*

165

N

is for...

Nitty Gritty

167

English	Spanish	German

Nah
[nah]
Slang for no.

Nelson; no
[nel-son; no]

Nä
[neh]

Nail
[nayl]
Catch someone.

Coger
[koh-her]

Jmdn. festnageln
[yeh-man-den fest-nah-geln]

Narc
[nahrk]
Abbreviation for member of the police specialising in narcotics arrests.

Policía anti-narco
[po-lee-see-ah an-tee-nar-ko]

Chloroformierer
[klo-ro-for-mee-rah]

Nasty
[nah-sstee]
Disgusting.

Antipático, -a
[an-tee-pah-tee-ko, -kah]

Eklig
[ek-leesh]

Nebbish
[neh-bish]
Someone easily overlook, a nonentity.

Invisible
[in-vee-see-blay]

Unwesen
[oon-veh-zen]

Neck
[nehk]
To kiss.

Beso
[beh-sow]

Knutschen
[knoot-shen]

Nerd
[nehrd]
Someone who doesnít know whatís going on and is socially inept.

Empollón
[em-po-yone]

Tölpel
[tool-pel]

French	Dutch	Japanese
Que dalle! *[keh dahl]*	**Noop** *[noh-oop]*	あかん *[ah-kahn]*
Agrafer *[aah-grah-fehr]*	**In de kraag grijpen** *[ihn deh kraachk chkrah-ee-pehn]*	パクる *[bah-koo-loo]*
Agent des stups *[ah-shent dehs stoohp]*	**Nark** *[nahrk]*	麻薬課 *[mah-yah-koo-kah]*
Déguelasse *[deh-gohl-ahss]*	**Smerig** *[ss-me-rehchk]*	汚らわしい *[keh-gah-lah-vah-shee]*
Cloche *[klosh]*	**Nul** *[neh-ohl]*	ろくでなし *[lo-koo-deh-nah-shee]*
Se bécorer *[seh beh-koh-reh]*	**Tongen** *[tohn-gehn]*	キスする *[kee-soo-soo-loo]*
Crétin *[kreh-tahn]*	**Lulletje rozewater** *[loo-leh-tje hrohze vah-tehr]*	くず *[koo-zoo]*

English	Spanish	German

Nick
[nihk]
To take or steal.

Chorizear
[cho-ree-seh-ar]

Mitgehen lassen
[meet-gayen las-sen]

Nickel
[nih-kehl]
Five dollar bag of drugs, usually marijuana.

Paco de cinco dólares
[pah-ko de sin-ko doe-lar-es]

Piecel
[pee-kehl]

Nickel and dime
[nih-kehl ahnd dym]
Someone who is cheap.

Barato, -a
[bah-rah-tow]

Für´n Appel und´n Ei zu haben
[fearn ap-pel unden ai tsu hah-ben]

Nigger
[nih-gah]
Derogatory slang for a black person.

Negro
[neh-grow]

Schwarzer
[shvahr-tsa]

NIMBY
[nihm-bee]
Acronym for "not in my backyard." Movement opposed to social programs, such as homeless shelelters, drug rehab, etc. in your neighborhood.

De derechas
[deh deh-reh-chahs]

Nicht mein Bierchen
[neesht mayn beer-shen]

French	Dutch	Japanese
Faucher *[foh-shehr]*	**Jatten** *[ee-ah-tehn]*	パクる *[pah-koo-loo]*
Une dose à cinq dollars *[oon-eh dohs ah sahnk doh-lahrs]*	**Een joetje stuff** *[ehn ee-ootje ss-tehph]*	ジ- *[jee]*
Pauvre bougre *[pohvr booh-greh]*	**Goedkoop** *[chkoot-koh-oop]*	けち *[keh-chee]*
Bougnol *[boo-niohl]*	**Nikker** *[nih-kehr]*	黒人 *[koh-koo-jeen]*
Les p'tits bourgeois *[lehp tiht boohr-shuah]*	**Niet op mijn stoep** *[niht ohp mah-een ss-toop]*	知ったこっちゃあない *[see-tah-ko-chah-nai]*

English	Spanish	German

Nitpicker
[niht-pih-kehr]
Someone who
concentrates on
minor technicalities
and minuta.

Exigente
[ex-ee-hen-tay]

**Kleinlicher
Mensch**
*[klai-nee-shah
mensh]*

Nitty-gritty
[niht-tee griht-tee]
Reality. The
bottom line.

La realidad
[la ray-ah-lee-dad]

**Der harte
Boden der
Tatsachen**
*[der har-teh bow-
den
der tat-za-chen]*

Nix
[nihkss]
To hinder or
prevent. To say no.

Corta
[kohr-tah]

Nix da
[nix-dah]

No-goodnik
[noh-good-nihk]
*Someone undesir-
able.*

Indeseable
*[in-deh-say-ah-
blay]*

**Persona non
grata**
*[per-zo-nah nohn
gra-tah]*

No no
[noh noh]
Social blunder.

Impertinencia
*[im-per-tee-nen-see-
ah]*

**Einen
Fauxpas
begehen**
*[ai-nen faux-pas
beh-geyen]*

Nooky
[nuh-kee]
To fool around
sexually.

Ligar
[lee-gar]

Rammeln
[ram-meln]

French	Dutch	Japanese
Couper les cheveux en quatre *[koop-eh leh sheh-veh ahn cahtr]*	**Kommaneuker** *[koh-mah-neh-oo-kehr]*	あら捜し屋 *[ah-lah-sah-gah-shee-yah]*
L'essentiel sans le baratin *[leh-sehn-see-ahl sahn leh bah-rah-tahn*	**De clou** *[deh kloo]*	核心 *[kah-koo-sheen]*
Pas mêche! *[pah mehsh]*	**Niks-nop-nul** *[nix-nohp-neh-ohl]*	ブ- *[boo]*
Bon à rien *[bohn ah ree-ahn]*	**Klootzak** *[klo-oot-zahk]*	駄目な奴 *[dah-meh-nah-yah-tsoo]*
Faux-pas *[foh pah]*	**Afgang** *[ahf-chkang]*	ボケ *[bo-keh]*
Crampe *[crahmp]*	**Rondneuken** *[hrohnd-neh-oo-kehn]*	プレ-ボ- イする *[play-boy-soo-roo]*

English	Spanish	German
Nosh *[nahsh]* To snack.	**Comer un aperitivo** *[ko-mer oon ah-peh-ree-tee-vo*	**Fressen** *[fres-sen]*
No way *[noh way]* Abbreviation for impossible	**Ni cagando** *[nee kah-gahn-doh]*	**Nix zu machen** *[nix tsu mah-chen]*
Nowhere *[noh-wayr]* Useless, a dead end, i.e. nowhere job.	**Sin salida** *[sin sahl-ee-dah]*	**Sysiphus-Arbeit** *[tzi-phoos-ar-byte]*
Number *[nuhm-behr]* Understand what someone wants, i.e. I´ve got his number.	**Tener señalado** *[teh-ner say-nya-lah-doh]*	**Jmdm. auf den Trichter kommen** *[yeh-man-dem owf den trish-tah kom-men]*
Number one *[nuhm-behr wuhn]* Urinate.	**Mear** *[may-ar]*	**Wasser abschlagen** *[vah-sah ab-shlah-gen]*
Number two *[nuhm-ber too]* Defecate.	**Cagar** *[cah-gar]*	**Koten** *[kot-ten]*
Nuts *[nuhtz]* Testicles.	**Cojones** *[ko-ho-nes]*	**Nüsse** *[noo-seh]*

French	Dutch	Japanese
Boulotter *[booh-loh-tehr]*	**Een vette bek halen** *[ehn veh-teh behk haah-lehn]*	つまむ *[tsoo-mah-moo]*
Pas question *[pah kehs-tee-ohn]*	**Rot op!** *[hroht ohp]*	無理 *[moo-lee]*
Un cul-de-sac *[ahn coold sahc]*	**Klotebaan** *[kloh-oo-teh-baahn]*	行き詰まり *[ee-kee-zoo-mah-ree]*
Branchér *[brahn-sheh]*	**Gesnopen** *[chkehs-noh-oo-pehn]*	がってん *[gah-ten]*
Pisser *[pee-seh]*	**Pissen** *[peehs-sehn]*	小 *[shoh]*
Chier *[shee-eh]*	**Beren** *[beh-ee-hrehn]*	大 *[dai]*
Les couilles *[leh coo-eeh-ieh]*	**Ballen** *[bohl-lehn]*	金玉 *[keen-tah-mah]*

O

is for...

Oaf

English	Spanish	German
Oaf *[ohf]* Clumsey.	**Menso, -a** *[men-so, -sah]*	**Plump** *[ploomp]*
O.D. *[oh-dee]* Abbreviation for overdose.	**Sobredosis** *[so-bray-doh-sees]*	**Überdosis** *[ee-bah-doh-zis]*
Oddball *[ahd-bahl]* Someone strange.	**Extraño** *[ex-trah-nyo]*	**Sonderling** *[zon-deh-ling]*
Off *[ohff]* *Kill someone.*	**Eliminar** *[eh-lee-mee-nar]*	**Aus** *[ows]*
Old lady *[ohld lay-dee]* Wife or girlfriend.	**Vieja** *[vee-eh-hah]*	**Alte** *[al-teh]*
Old man *[ohld mahn]* Husband or boyfriend.	**Viejo** *[vee-eh-ho]*	**Alter** *[al-tah]*
Oreo *[oh-ree-oh]* Derogatory for black person who acts white. From Oreo cookie, a cookie with white cream between two chocolate disks.	**Negro enblanquecido** *[nay-gro en-blan- kay-see-doh]*	**Überanpasser** *[ee-bah-on-pas-sah]*

French	Dutch	Japanese
Andouille [ahn-doo-eeh-ieh]	**Ezel** [eh-ee-zehl]	うすのろ [oo-soo-no-loh]
Overdose [oh- vehr-dohs]	**O.D.** [oh-oo deh-ee]	ヤクのやりすぎ [yah-koo-no-yah-lee-soo-gee]
Farfelu [fahr-feh-looh]	**Mafkees** [mahf-keh-ees]	変人奇人 [hen-geen-kee-geen]
Descendre quelqu'un [deh-sehndr]	**Iemand koud maken** [ee-mahnd kah-oot maah-kehn]	消す [keh-soo]
La patrone [lah pah-trohn]	**M'n meissie** [mehn mah-ee-see]	人妻 [hee-toh-zoo-mah]
Le patron [leh pah-trohn]	**M'n vent** [mehn vehnt]	夫 [oh-toh]
Un éclair [ahn eh-clehr]	**Negerzoen** [neh-ee-chkehr-zoon]	白人気取りの黒人 [hah-koo-jeen-kee-doh-lee-no-ko-koo-jeen]

English	Spanish	German

Over the top
[oh-ver thah tahp]
Outrageous
behavior.

Sensacionalista
[sen-sah-see-o-na-lees-tah]

Üeber die Höhe
[ee-bah dee hoo-eh]

Out
[owht]
To expose
someoneís homo-
sexuality.

Abrirse
[ah-brear-say]

Jmdn. outen
[yeh-man-den ow-ten]

Out of the closet
[owht uhv thah klah-zeht]
Openly homo-
sexual.

Homosexual declarado
[ho-mo-sex-u-al deh-cla-ra-doh]

Schwule Sau
[shvoo-leh zow]

French	Dutch	Japanese
Excessif *[x-seh-seef]*	**Krankjorem** *[krohnk-ee-oh-hrehm]*	暴行 *[bo-koh]*
Se découvrir *[she deh-cooh-vrihr]*	**Uit de kast komen** *[ah-oot deh kohst koh-oo-mehn]*	ホモだとばらす *[ho-mo-dah-toh-bah-lah-soo]*
S'avouer *[sah-vooh-ehr]*	**Uit de kast** *[ah-oot deh kohst]*	オプンホモ *[oh-poon-ho-mo]*

P

is for...

Pusher

English	Spanish	German

Pad
[pahd]
Home or apartment.

Casa
[kah-sah]

Bude
[boo-deh]

Pan
[pahn]
A bad review.

Mala reseña
[mah-lah reh-say-nya]

Jmdn. in die Pfanne hauen
[yeh-man-den in dee fan-neh how-wen]

Party
[pahr-tee]
To do drugs.

Juerga
[hweh-gah]

Fette
[feh-teh]

Patsy
[paht-see]
Fall guy. Someone who is a loser.

Pobre diablo
[po-bray dee-ah-blow]

Verlierer
[fehr-lee-rah]

Pay-off
[pay ohff]
Reward.

Recompensa
[reh-com-pen-sah]

Belohnung
[beh-low-noong]

Pecker
[peh-kehr]
Penis.

Polla
[po-yah]

Piller
[pee-lah]

Pecs
[pehkss]
Abbreviation for pectoral muscles.

Pecho
[peh-cho]

Schließmuskel
[shlees-moos-kel]

Pee
[pee]
Urinate.

Hacer pipi
[a-ser pee-pee]

Pissen
[pees-sen]

French	Dutch	Japanese
Une piaule *[oon-eh peeh-ohl]*	**Stekie** *[ss-teh-kee]*	家 *[ee-yeh]*
Déglingade *[deh-glahn-gahd]*	**Kutkritieken** *[kooht-khree-tee-kehn]*	悪評 *[ah-koo-hyoh]*
S'éclater *[seh-clah-teh]*	**Gebruiken** *[chkeh-bhrah-oo-kehn]*	薬をやる *[koo-soo-ree oh yah-loo]*
Un raté *[ahn rah-teh]*	**Loser** *[loh-oo-sehr]*	かも *[kah-moh]*
Bourse *[boohrs]*	**Kat in 't bakkie** *[kaht ihn-eht bah-kee]*	報酬 *[ho-shoo]*
Zob *[zohb]*	**Leuter** *[leh-oo-tehr]*	ぽこちん *[po-ko-chin]*
Pecs *[pehcs]*	**Wasbord** *[vahs-bohrt]*	胸 *[moo-neh]*
La pisse *[lah pihs]*	**Lekken** *[leh-kehn]*	おしっこ *[oh-shee-ko]*

English	Spanish	German
Pen [pehn] Prison.	**Chirona** [chee-ro-nah]	**Knast** [knast]
Perp [pehrp] Police jargon for perpetrator of a crime.	**Criminal** [cri-mee-nal]	**Krimineller** [kree-mee-nel-lah]
Perv [pehrv] Abbreviation for pervert.	**Pervertido** [per-ver-tee-doh]	**Pervers** [per-vers]
Piece [peess] A gun or abbreviation for ìpiece of assî (sexy woman).	**Pipa** [pee-pah]	**Weibsstück** [vibe-shtook]
Pig [pihg] Derogatory for unattractive woman.	**Cerda** [ther-dah]	**Sau** [zow]
Pig out [pihg owht] Overeat.	**Jalar** [hah-lar]	**Überfressen** [ee-bah-fres-sen]
Pimp [pihmp] Someone who controls prostitutes.	**Chulo ; cafishio** [choo-low; ka-fee-see-oh]	**Zuhälter** [tsoo-chel-tah]

French	Dutch	Japanese
La taule *[lah tohl]*	**Lik** *[lehk]*	務所 *[moo-sho]*
Un criminel *[ahn kree-mee-nehl]*	**V.d.** *[veh-ee deh-ee]*	ホシ *[ho-shee]*
Un vieux salaud *[ahn vee-eh sah-loh]*	**Vieserik** *[vee-seh-reek]*	変質者 *[hen-shee-tsoo-shah]*
Un canon *[ahn kah-nohn]*	**Lekker ding** *[lehk-kehr dihng]*	ピストル *[pee-soo-toh-loo]*
Un treux *[ahn treh]*	**Monster** *[mohn-ster]*	ブス *[boo-soo]*
Se goinfrer *[seh goo-ahn-freh]*	**Volvreten** *[vohl-vreh-ee-tehn]*	食べ過ぎ *[tah-beh-soo-gee]*
Un mac *[ahn mahc]*	**Pooier** *[poh-ee-ee-ehr]*	ポン引き *[pohn-bee-kee]*

English	Spanish	German
Pimpmobile *[pihmp-moh-beel]* Flashy car.	**Carro de chulo** *[kar-ro de choo-low]*	**Schlitten** *[shlee-ten]*
Pinch *[pihnch]* Seal something.	**Pellizco** *[peh-yeez-ko]*	**Klemmen** *[klem-men]*
Pinko *[peen-koh]* Derogatory for communist.	**Rojo** *[ro-ho]*	**Roter** *[ro-tah]*
Pisher *[pee-shehr]* A youngster. (Yiddish for urinate) someone who wets the bed.	**Mearse en la cama** *[may-ar-seh en la kah-mah]*	**Bettpisser** *[bet-pee-sah]*
Piss off *[pihss ohff]* Please,go away.	**Que te den por el culo** *[keh teh den por el koo-lo]*	**Verpiß dich** *[fehr-pees deesh]*
Pisser *[pihss-ssehr]* A funny joke or situation.	**Chiste** *[chees-teh]*	**Bepisser** *[beh-pee-sah]*
Plastered *[plah-stehrd]* Extremely intoxicated.	**Estar pedo** *[es-tar peh-doh]*	**Hackebreit** *[chah-keh-brite]*

French	Dutch	Japanese
Une voiture de mac *[oon-eh vooh-ah-toohr deh mahc]*	Pooierbak *[poh-ee-ee-ehr-bohk]*	ハデな車 *[hah-deh-nah-koo-roo-mah]*
Piquer *[pee-keh]*	Jatten *[ee-ah-tehn]*	つねる *[tsoo-neh-loo]*
Un coco *[ahn coh-coh]*	Rooie *[rah-oo-ee-eh]*	アカ *[ah-kah]*
Un pisseur *[ahn peeh-sehr]*	Bedpisser *[beht-pees-sehr]*	小便小僧 *[shoh-ben-ko-zoh]*
Tire-toi! *[teer-too-ah]*	Teer op *[teh-ehr ohp]*	失せろ *[oo-seh-loh]*
Une bonne vanne *[oon-eh bohn vahn]*	Een giller *[ehn chkeeh-lehr]*	冗談 *[jo-dahn]*
Bourré *[boo-rheh]*	Strontbezopen *[ss-throhnt-beh-zoh-oo-pehn]*	泥酔 *[day-soo-ee]*

English	Spanish	German

Plotz
[plahtz]
State of exaustion.

Estar muerto, -a
[es-tar mwer-toh, -tah]

Danach
[dah-nach]

Poke
[pohk]
Sexual intercourse.

Ligar
[lee-gar]

Stoß
[shtose]

Polack
[poh-lahk]
Derogatory for Polish.

Polaco
[po-lah-ko]

Pollacke
[poe-lah-keh]

Polluted
[poh-loo-tehd]
Drunk.

Estar pedo
[es-tar peh-do]

Kontaminiert
[kon-tah-mee-nee-yert]

Poop
[poop]
To defecate.

Hacer caca
[ah-ser kah-kah]

Kacken
[kah-ken]

Pooper-scooper
[poo-pehr-skoo-pehr]
Implement to clean a dogís feces. In some places there are "Pooper Scooper" laws requiring this.

Recoge-caca
[reh-ko-hay kah-kah]

Hundedreck
[hoon-deh-drek]

Pot
[paht]
Abbreviation for marijuana.

Hierba
[yee-er-bah]

Etwas zu bauen
[et-vahs tsoo bow-en]

French	Dutch	Japanese
Crevé *[creh-veh]*	**Afgepeigerd** *[ahf-chkeh-pah-ee-chkeht]*	くたくた *[koo-tah-koo-tah]*
Une nique *[oon-eh neek]*	**Naaien** *[nah-ee-ehn]*	セックスする *[seh-koo-soo-soo-roo]*
Polack *[poh-lahck]*	**Polak** *[poh-oo-lahk]*	ポランド人 *[poh-lan-doh-jeen]*
Démonté *[dhe-mohn-teh]*	**Bezopen** *[beh-zoh-oo-pehn]*	酔っ払う *[yo-pah-lah-oo]*
Raguer *(provençal) [rah-geh]*	**Schijten** *[ss-chkah-ee-tehn]*	ウンχする *[oon-chee-soo-loo]*
La moto-caca *[lah moh-toh-kah-kah]*	**Poepschepje** *[poohos-schkeh-pje]*	ウンコ取り *[oon-koh-toh-lee]*
L'herbe *[lerhb]*	**Stuff** *[ss-tehf]*	マリフアナ *[mah-ree-hoo-ah-nah]*

English	Spanish	German
Pot head *[paht hehd]* Habitual pot smoker.	**Marihuanero** *[ma-ree-wah-neh-ro]*	**Kiffer** *[kee-fah]*
Preppie *[preh-pee]* Derogatory for someone who attends prep school or dresses conservatively. A rich kid.	**Niño bien, pijo** *[nee-nyo bee-en, pee-ho]*	**Popper** *[poe-pah]*
Prick *[prihk]* Penis. Someone who is mean.	**Polla** *[po-yah]*	**Pisser** *[pee-sah]*
Psycho *[sy-koh]* Abbreviation for psychopath. Crazy.	**Sicópata** *[see-ko-pah-tah]*	**Psychopath** *[psee-cho-paht]*
Puke *[pyook]* Vomit.	**Vomitar** *[vo-mee-tar]*	**Erbrechen** *[ehr-breh-chen]*
Punk *[puhnk]* Fan of "Punk" rock. Usually,teenagagers with mohawk hairstyles, tatoos, torn clothing, pierced body parts, and garishly colored hair.	**Punk** *[poonk]*	**Punk** *[pahnk]*

French	Dutch	Japanese
Un fumeur d'herbe *[ahn foo-mehr dehrb]*	**Hashjhoofd** *[hahsh-ho-ooft]*	はっぱ中 *[hah-pah-choo]*
BCBG (Bon Chic Bon Genre) *[beh-seh-beh-sheh]*	**Balletje** *[bahl-leh-tje]*	金持ちのガキ *[kah-neh-mo-chee no gah-kee]*
Un bitard *[ahn beet-ahrd]*	**Lul** *[leh-ohl]*	ペニス *[peh-nee-soo]*
Un marteau *[ahn mahr-toh]*	**Gestoorde** *[chkehs-tohr-deh]*	気違い *[kee-chee-gai]*
Dégueuler *[deh-geh-leh]*	**Kots** *[kohts]*	ゲロ *[geh-roh]*
Kpun *[keh-pahn]*	**Punk** *[pehnk]*	パンク *[pahn-koo]*

English	Spanish	German
Pusher *[puh-shehr]* Drug dealer.	**Camello** *[kah-meh-yo]*	**Drogenhändler** *[droe-gen-hehn-dlah]*
Pussy *[puh-see]* Female genitals.	**Coñito** *[ko-nyee-toh]*	**Muschi** *[moo-shee]*
Pussy-whipped *[puh-see wihpt]* Man who is dominated by a woman.	**Calzonudo** *[kal-zo-noo-doh]*	**Pantoffelheld** *[pan-toe-fell-cheld]*
Put out *[puht-owht]* Woman who permits man to have sexual intercourse with her.	**Mujer fácil** *[moo-herr fah-seel]*	**Ausziehdame** *[ows-tseech-dam-meh]*
Pyro *[py-roh]* Abbreviation for pyromaniac.	**Piromano** *[pee-ro-mah-no]*	**Feuerteufel** *[foe-yah-toy-fell]*

French	Dutch	Japanese
Un dealer *[ahn deeh-lehr]*	**Dealer** *[dee-lehr]*	売人 *[bai-neen]*
La foufoune *[lah foo-foohn]*	**Flamoes** *[flah-moos]*	アソコ *[ah-so-ko]*
Un fil-doux *[ahn fee-dooh]*	**Onder de plak** *[ohn-dehr deh plahk]*	尻しかれ *[shee-lee-shee-kah-reh]*
Une femme facile *[oon-eh fehm fah-seehl]*	**Sletje** *[ss-leh-tje]*	セックスフレンド *[seh-koo-soo-hoo-len-doh]*
Un pyromane *[ahn pee-roh-mahn]*	**Pyromaan** *[pee-roh-mahn]*	放火魔 *[ho-kah-mah]*

Q

is for...

Queer

197

English	Spanish	German
Q.T. *[kyoo-tee]* Abbreviation for secret.	**Pecreto** *[seh-cree-to]*	**VS geheim** *[vee es geh-chaim]*
Quack *[kwahk]* Derogatory for medical doctor. An imposter	**Matasanos** *[mah-tah-sah-nos]*	**Quacksalber** *[kvak-zal-bah]*
Queen *[kween]* An effeminate homosexual.	**Travesti** *[trah-ves-tee]*	**Tunte** *[toon-teh]*
Queer *[kweehr]* A homosexual.	**Marica** *[mah-ree-kah]*	**Arschficker** *[arsh-fee-kah]*
Queer bashing *[kweehr bah-sheen]* To assault someone becuase they are homosexual.	**Cazar maricones** *[kah-thar mah-ree-ko-nes]*	**Schwulen Klatschen** *[shfoo-len klat-tshen]*

French	Dutch	Japanese
Endouée *[ahn-doo-eh]*	**Geheimpie** *[chkeh-haa-eem-pee]*	エス *[eh-soo]*
Un charlatan *[ahn shahr-lah-tahn]*	**Oplichter** *[ohp-leechk-tehr]*	やぶ医者 *[yah-boo-ee-shah]*
Une folle *[oon-eh foh-leh]*	**Nicht** *[neechkt]*	おかま *[oh-kah-mah]*
Un pédé *[ahn peh-deh]*	**Poot** *[poh-oot]*	ホモ *[ho-mo]*
Chasse aux pédés *[shas oh peh-deh]*	**Potenrammer** *[poh-oot-ehn-hrah-mehr]*	ホモいじめ *[ho-mo-ee-jee-meh]*

R

is for...

Rubber

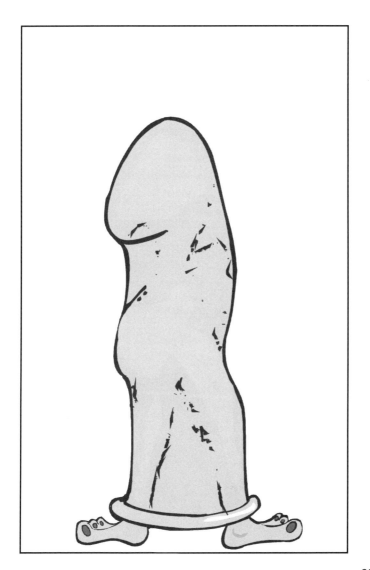

201

English	Spanish	German
Rad *[rahd]* Abbreviation for radical. Cool in vernacular of Valley Girl.	**¡De puta madre!** *[de poo-tah mah-dre]*	**Cool** *[koohl]*
Radical *[rah-dee-kuhl]* Cool.	**¡Cojonudo!** *[ko-ho-noo-doh]*	**Radikal** *[rah-dee-kal]*
Rag (on the) *[rahg]* Woman who is menstruating. Also derogatory for woman in a bad mood.	**Tener el tomate** *[teh-ner el toh-mah-teh]*	**Ihre Tage haben** *[ear-reh tah-geh hah-ben]*
Rap sheet *[rahp sheet]* A person's criminal history.	**Historial** *[his-toh-ree-al]*	**Kerbholz** *[kerb-choltz]*
Rat *[raht]* Unpleasant, dishonest person.	**Chivato** *[chee-vah-toh]*	**Ratte** *[rah-teh]*
Raunchy *[rawh-chee]* Dirty, sexually explicit, disgusting	**Vulgar** *[vul-gar]*	**Eklig** *[eh-kleesh]*
Ream *[reem]* To have sexual intercourse.	**Perforar** *[per-for-rar]*	**Vögeln** *[fih-geln]*

French	Dutch	Japanese
Cool *[coohl]*	**Waanzinnig** *[vah-aan-zeen-neechk]*	過激派 *[kah-geh-kee-hah]*
Super! *[sooh-pehr]*	**Heftig** *[hehf-techk]*	めちゃいい *[meh-chah-ee]*
Avoir ses ours *[ah-voo-ahr sehs oohrs]*	**Opoe** *[oh-oo-poo]*	ブルーデー *[boo-loo-deh]*
Un casier judiciaire *[ahn casee-ehr shu-dee-see-air]*	**Strafblad** *[ss-trahf-blaht]*	前科 *[zen-kah]*
Une ordure *[oon-eh ohr-door-eh]*	**Smeerlap** *[ss-mee-ehr-lahp]*	こそ泥 *[ko-so-doh-loh]*
Grivois *[gree-voo-ahs]*	**Ranzig** *[hrahn-zeeg]*	下品 *[geh-heen]*
Barrer *[bah-rher]*	**Rammen** *[hrah-mehn]*	押す *[oh-soo]*

English	Spanish	German

Rear
[reehr]
Buttocks.

Trasero
[trah-seh-roh]

Hinterteil
[heen-tah-tile]

Reefer
[ree-fehr]
Marijuana.

Marimba
[mah-reem-bah]

Gras
[grass]

Rehab
[re-hahb]
Abbreviation for
rehabilitation,
usually for people
with substance
abuse problems.

Rehabilitación
[re-ah-bee-lee-tah-see-on]

**Auf Entzug
sein**
[owf ent-tsook zain]

Retard
[ree-tahrd]
Abbreviation for
mentally retarded.
A stupid person.

Retardado
[reh-tar-dah-doh]

Armleuchter
[arm-loish-tah]

Ride
[ryd]
Sexual intercourse.

Tirar
[tee-rar]

Reiten
[rai-ten]

Rim
[rihm]
Generally homo-
sexual practice of
licking anus.

Lamer el culo
[la-mer el koo-loh]

Arschlecken
[arsh-leh-ken]

Rip off
[rihp ohff]
To steal or swindle.

Timar
[tee-mar]

Etwas reißen
[et-vas rai-sen]

French	Dutch	Japanese
Le cul *[leh coohl]*	**Billen** *[beel-lehn]*	尻 *[shee-lee]*
Un reefer *[ahn reeh-fehr]*	**Stuff** *[ss-toof]*	マリフアナ *[mah-ree-fah-nah]*
Réhab *[reh-ahb]*	**Reso** *[reh-ee-soh]*	リハビリ *[lee-hah-bee-lee]*
Un arrieré **áhn** *[ahn ah-ree-ehr-eh]*	**Halve gare** *[hah-ohl chkah-reh*	幼稚 *[yo-chee]*
S'énvoyer en **l'air** *[sahn-voo-ah-ee-ehr* *ahn lehr]*	**Ritje** *[hreet-tje]*	乗る *[no-loo]*
Faire feuille **de rose** *[fehr feh-oo-ee dhe* *rohs]*	**Kontlikken** *[kohnt-lee-kehn]*	肛門をなめる *[koh-mohn oh nah-* *meh-roo]*
Baiser la **geuil** *[beh-seh lah gehl]*	**Zwendelen** *[zvehn-deh-lehn]*	ねこばば *[neh-ko-bah-bah]*

English	Spanish	German
Roach [rohch] The butt of a marijuana cigarette.	**Chicharra** [chee-char-rah]	**Kippe eines Joint** [kee-peh ai-nes joint]
Roadie [roh-dee] Support staff for rock band.	**Forofo** [fo-ro-fo]	**Roadie** [row-dee]
Road hog [rohd- hohg] Large motorcycle, hog for short.	**Supermoto** [soo-per-mo-toh]	**Straßensau** [shtrah-sen-zow]
Rod [rahd] Penis.	**Miembro** [mee-em-bro]	**Johannes** [yo-hah-nes]
Rot gut [raht guht] Cheap liquor.	**Licor de quemar** [lee-kor de kay-mar]	**Fusel** [foo-zel]
Rubber [ruhb-behr] Condom.	**Goma** [go-mah]	**Gummi** [goo-mee]
Rub out [ruhb-owht] Assisinate.	**Eliminar** [eh-lee-mee-nar]	**Ausradieren** [ows-rad-ear-ren]
Rusky [roo-skee] Russian.	**Ruso, -a** [roo-so, -sa]	**Iwan** [ee-vahn]

French	Dutch	Japanese
Un mégot *[ahn meh-goh]*	**Kick** *[keeck]*	ハッパの吸い殻 *[hah-pah no soo-ee-gah-rah]*
Les roadies *[leh roh-deeh]*	**Roadie** *[roh-ah-dee]*	ロ-ディ *[loh-dee]*
Un sacré engin *[ahn sak-reh ehn-shihn]*	**Wegpiraat** *[vechk-pee-hrat]*	単車 *[tahn-shah]*
Matraque *[mah-thrahk]*	**Paal** *[pahl]*	ボウ *[boh]*
Un tord boyaux *[ahn tohr boh-ioh]*	**Rioolwater** *[ree-ohl-vah-tehr]*	安酒 *[yah-soo-zah-keh]*
Une capote *[ahn cah-poht]*	**Kapotje** *[kah-poh-tje]*	ゴム *[go-moo]*
Feigner *[feh-een-iehr]*	**Koud maken** *[kah-oot-mah-kehn]*	消す *[keh-soo]*
Un popol *[ahn poh-pohl]*	**Rooie beer** *[roh-oo-ee-eh behr]*	ロシア人 *[loh-shee-ah-jeen]*

207

S

is for...
Shit

English	Spanish	German

Sack
[sahk]
Bed.

Sobre
[so-breh]

Nest
[nest]

Saturday night special
[sah-tuhr-day nyt speh-shuhl]
A cheap handgun.

Cacharra
[kah-char-rah]

Knarre
[knah-reh]

Sauce
[sawhss]
Alcohol.

Trago
[trah-go]

Stoff
[shtowf]

S.B.D.
[ehss-bee-dee]
Abbreviation for a ìsilent but deadlyî fart.

Pedo asesino
[peh-doh ah-seh-see-no]

Stiller aber tödlicher Furz
[shtee-lah ah-bah tood-lee-shah foortz]

Scab
[skahb]
A worker who crosses a union picket line.

Cagado
[kah-gao-doh]

Streikbrecher
[shtraik-breh-shah]

Scam
[skahm]
A trick or swindle.

Estafa
[eh-stah-fah]

Betrug
[beh-troog]

Scalper
[skahl-pehr]
Someone who illegally sells tickets to performances.

Revendedor
[reh-ben-deh-door]

Schwarzhändler von Eintrittskarten
[shvartz-hand-lah fone ain-treets-kar-ten]

French	Dutch	Japanese
Un pieu *[ahn pieh]*	**Nest** *[nehst]*	サック *[sah-koo]*
Un flingue *[ahn fleeng]*	**Proppeschieter** *[phrohp-peh-schkeet-tehr]*	安いピストル *[yah-soo-ee-pee-soo-toh-loo]*
Le picole *[leh pee-cohl]*	**Drank** *[dhrahnk]*	さけ *[sah-keh]*
Un foireux *[ahn fooah-ree-eh]*	**Sluiper** *[ss-lah-oo-pehr]*	透かしっぺ *[soo-kah-she-peh]*
Un jaune *[ahnshohn]*	**Bal gehakt** *[bahl chkeh-hahkt]*	ストやぶり *[soo-toh-yah-boo-ree]*
Une arnaque *[oon-eh ahr-nahq]*	**Zwendeltruukje** *[z-vehn-dehl-throokje]*	詐欺 *[sah-gee]*
Un empileur *[ahn ehm-pee-lehr]*	**Zwarthandelaar** *[z-vahrt-hahn-dehl-aahr]*	ダフ屋 *[dah-foo-yah]*

English	Spanish	German
Schizo *[skih-tzoh]* Abbreviation for schizophrenic. Someone who has wild and unexpected mood swings.	**Pirado** *[pee-rah-doh]*	**Schizo** *[schee-zoe]*
Schlemiel *[shlih-meel]* Clumsey person.	**Torpe** *[shleh-mee-ehl]*	**Schlemihl** *[shleh-meel]*
Schlep *[shlehp]* To carry something.	**Cargar** *[car-gar]*	**Schleppen** *[shlehp-pen]*
Schlock *[shlahk]* Cheap merchandise.	**Baratijas** *[bah-rah-tee-hahs]*	**Billiger Jakob** *[bee-lee-gah yah-kob]*
Schlong *[shlahng]* Penis.	**Rabo** *[rah-bo]*	**Schwengel** *[shven-gel]*
Schlump *[shluhmp]* Sloppy.	**Un pintas** *[oon peen-tahs]*	**Schlampig** *[shlem-peesh]*
Schmaltz *[shmahltz]* Overly sentimental.	**Cursi** *[koor-see]*	**Schmalzig** *[shmal-tseesh]*
Scram *[skrahm]* Get away.	**Largarse** *[lar-gar-seh]*	**Abhauen** *[ab-chow-en]*

French	Dutch	Japanese
Siphonné *[ahn see-pho-neh]*	**Schizo** *[ss-chkeet-tzo]*	精神分裂症 *[say-sheen-boon-leh-tsoo-shoh]*
Une gourde *[oon-eh goor-deh]*	**Schlemiel** *[ss-leh-meel]*	鈍 *[dohn]*
Trimballer *[trihm-bah-ier]*	**Slepen** *[ss-leh-ee-pehn]*	運ぶ *[hah-ko-boo]*
Camelotte *[cah-mehl-oht]*	**Prullaria** *[phrooh-lah-ree-ah]*	安もん *[yah-soo-mohn]*
voir "PENIS"	**Slang** *[ss-lahng]*	男根 *[dahn-kohn]*
Pagailleux *[pah-gah-ieh]*	**Morsig** *[mohr-seechk]*	あかんたれ *[ah-kahn-tah-leh]*
Guimauve *[gih-mohv]*	**Zoetsappig** *[zoot-sahp-pehchk]*	おセン χ *[oh-sehn-chee]*
Se tirer *[seh tee-reh]*	**'M smeren** *[ehm ss-meer-ehn]*	とっとと失せろ *[toh-toh-toh-oo-seh-loh]*

213

English	Spanish	German

Screamer
[skree-mehr]
Woman who makes loud noises during sexual intercourse.

Escandalosa
[es-kan-dah-low-sah]

Schreierin
[shrai-eh-reen]

Screw
[skroo]
Have sexual intercourse.

Tirarse a alguien
[tee-rar-seh a al-gee-en]

Poppen
[poe-pen]

Scumbag
[skum-bahg]
A rotten person.

Jodido; cagado
[cho-dee-doh; kah-gah-doh]

Abschaum
[ab-shaum]

Scuzzy
[skuh-zee]
Dirty.

Asqueroso, -a
[ass-keh-ro-so]

Dreckig
[dreh-keesh]

Set-up
[seht-uhp]
A trick.

Truco
[troo-ko]

Trick
[treek]

Sex kitten
[sehkss kih-tehn]
Sensual young girl, i.e. Ann Margaret.

Gatita
[gah-tee-tah]

Ficknelke
[feek-nel-keh]

Shack-up
[shahk-uhp]
Cohabitate.

Convivir
[kon-vee-vir]

Brockenzusammenschmeißen
[broe-ken-tsoo-zah-men-shmai-sen]

Shaft (get the)
[shahft]
To be taken advantage of or abused.

Pasarse de huevón
[pah-sah-seh de hwe-von]

In den Griff kriegen
[in den greef kree-gen]

French	Dutch	Japanese
Une hurleuse *[ooneh oor-lehs]*	**Gilneukertje** *[chkeel-noh-oo-kehr-tje]*	スクリ-マ- *[soo-koo-lee-mah]*
Prendre *[prahndr]*	**Naaien** *[nah-ee-ehn]*	セックスする *[seh-koo-soo-soo-loo]*
Une peigne-cul *[oon-eh pain-ie coohl]*	**Hufter** *[hef-tehr]*	腐った野郎 *[koo-sah-tah-yah-loh*
Dégueulasse *[deh-gohl-ahs]*	**Vunzig** *[voon-tzehchk]*	ババちい *[bah-bah-chee]*
Un coup monté *[ahn koop mohn-teh]*	**Truukje** *[throokje]*	企み *[tah-koo-mee]*
Une petite chatte *[oon-eh peh-teet shaht]*	**Sexpoesje** *[seks-poosje]*	セクシ少女 *[seh-koo-shee-shoh-joh]*
Se mettre à la colle *[seh meht-reh ah lah cohl]*	**Hokken** *[hohk-kehn]*	同棲する *[doh-say-soo-loo]*
Se faire enculer *[seh fehr ahn-cool-ehr]*	**Genaaid zijn** *[chkeh-nah-eed zah-een]*	カモになる *[kah-moh-nee-nah-roo]*

English	Spanish	German

Shiner
[shy-nehr]
Black eye.

Moretón
[moh-reh-tone]

Limo
[lee-moe]

Shit
[shiht]
Literally means
feces. Expression of
disgust or dismay.

Mierda
[mee-er-dah]

Scheiße
[shai-seh]

Shit-faced
[shiht-faysst]
Inebreated.

Estar pedo
[es-tar pay-doh]

Blaß
[blahs]

Shit kickers
[shiht kih-kehrz]
Large, heavy shoes.

Zapatones
[zah-pah-toe-nes]

Treter
[treh-tah]

Shit-list
[shiht-lihsst]
A person whoís
done someone
wrong in some way,
figuratively
goes on this list.

Lista negra
[lees-tah neh-grah]

Scheißliste
[shais-lees-teh]

Shrimp
[shrihmp]
A small person.

Enano, -a
[eh-nah-no]

Knirps
[knearps]

Shtup
[shtuhp]
To have sexual
intercourse.

Meter
[meh-ter]

Steigen
[shtai-gen]

216

French	Dutch	Japanese
L'oeil au beure noir *[loh-eh-ihl oh behr noo-ahr]*	**Een blauwe** *[ehn blah-oo-eh]*	くま *[koo-mah]*
Merde *[mehrd]*	**Schijt** *[ss-chkah-eet]*	クソ *[koo-so]*
Bourré *[booh-rheh]*	**Uit je roer raken** *[ah-oot ee-eh hroor hrah-kehn]*	バカづら *[bah-kah-zoo-lah]*
Des écrases-merdes *[dhes ehk-rahss mehrds]*	**Kistjes** *[kees-shehs]*	どたぐつ *[doh-tah-goo-tsoo]*
La liste noire *[lah leehst noo-ahr]*	**Zwarte lijst** *[z-vahrt-eh lah-eest]*	ブラックリスト *[boo-lah-koo-lee-stoh]*
Un avorton *[ahn ah-bohr tohn]*	**Onderdeur** *[ohn-dehr-dehr]*	χビ *[chee-bee]*
voir "FUCK"	**Iemand een beurt geven** *[ee-mahnd ehn behrt chkeh-ee-vehn]*	セックスする *[seh-koo-soo-soo-loo]*

English	Spanish	German

Shyster
[shy-sstehr]
A crook, usually a lawyer.

Estafador
[es-tah-fah-dor]

Gauner
[gow-nah]

Skid row
[skihd roh]
Bad neighboorhood, ususally place where homeless alcoholics congregate.

Tugurio
[too-goo-ree-oh]

Pennerheim
[peh-nah-chaim]

Skivies
[skih-veez]
Underwear.

Bragas
[brah-gas]

Unterwäsche
[oon-tah-veh-sheh]

Slammer
[slahm-mehr]
Prison.

Cárcel
[kar-sell]

Knast
[khn-ost]

Sleazy
[slee-zee]
Rotten and under-handed.

Sopla pollas
[soh-plah poh-yaass]

Verkommen und hinterhältig
[fehr-kohm-men oond heen-ter-chel-teesh]

Slit
[sliht]
The vulva.

Raja
[rah-ha]

Muschi
[moo-shee]

Smack
[smahk]
Heroin.

Jaco
[ha-coh]

Hera
[cheh-rah]

French	Dutch	Japanese
Un avocat veteux *[ahn ah-voh-caht veh-teh]*	**Schoft** *[ss-chkoft]*	いんちき弁護士 *[in-chee-kee-ben-go-shee]*
La zone *[lah sohn]*	**Achterbuurt** *[achk-tehr-boohrt]*	どや街 *[do-yah-gai]*
Caleçons *[cahl-sohss]*	**Ondergoed** *[ohn-dehr-chkoot]*	下着 *[shee-tah-gee]*
En taule *[ahn tohl]*	**Bajes** *[bah-ee-ehs]*	務所 *[moo-shoh]*
Sordide *[sohr-didh]*	**Achterbaks** *[ach-tehr-bahks]*	不良 *[foo-ryoh]*
La fente *[lah fehnt]*	**Spleetje** *[ss-pleh-ee-tje]*	さけめ *[sah-keh-meh]*
Smack *[ss-mahc]*	**Bolletje bruin** *[bohl-leh-tje brhrah-oon]*	ブツ *[boo-tsoo]*

English	Spanish	German
Smart-ass *[smahrt- ahss]* Someone cocky and obnoxious.	**Zorro hijo de puta** *[zoh-rroh e-ho the pu-tah]*	**Austößig** *[ows-shtuh-sheesh]*
Snafu *[snah-foo]* Military term that stands for "situation normal, all fucked up." A problem.		**Alles im Eimer** *[ahles ihm aih-mah]*
Snatch *[snahch]* Female genitalia.	**Jodido** *[ho-dee-doh]*	**Objekt der Begierde** *[o-bee-yekt der beh-gear-deh]*
Snit *[sniht]* In a bad mood.	**Mala leche** *[mah-lah leh-cheh]*	**Schlechte Laune** *[shlesh-teh lau-neh]*
Snitch *[snihch]* Someone who passes along secret information for gain.	**Soplón** *[soh-plon]*	**Verräter** *[fehr-reh-tah]*
Snot *[snaht]* Nasal mucus. Someone who is snobbish.	**Moco** *[moh-coh]*	**Popel** *[poe-pell]*
Snow *[snoh]* Cocaine.	**Blanca** *[blan-kah]*	**Koks** *[koks]*

French	Dutch	Japanese
Fortiche *[fohr-tihsh]*	**Goochemerd** *[chkoh-oo-chkeh-mehrt]*	いやな奴 *[ee-yah-nah-yah-tsoo]*
Amoché *[ah-moh-sheh]*	**Sores** *[ss-oh-hrehs]*	おわり *[oh-wah-ree]*
Baba *[bah-bah]*	**Muts** *[mehts]*	オマンコ *[oh-mahn-ko]*
Rogne *[rhogn]*	**Chagrijnig** *[schachk-heh-hrah-ee-nechk]*	暗い *[koo-lai]*
Un cafard *[ahn cah-fahrd]*	**Verrader** *[veh-hrad-dehr]*	ちくり屋 *[chee-koo-ree-yah]*
Morve *[mohrv]*	**Snot** *[ss-noht]*	きどり屋 *[kee-doh-ree-yah]*
La neige *[nehsh]*	**Bolletje wit** *[bohl-leht-tje veht]*	ユキ *[yoo-kee]*

English	Spanish	German
S.O.B. *[ehss-oh-bee]* Abbreviation for Son Of a Bitch.	**Hijo de puta** *[ee-yo de poo-tah]*	**Hurensohn** *[hoor-ren-zohn]*
Spaced-out *[spaysst-owht]* Someone who has their head in the clouds, not paying attention. Someone high on drugs.	**Despistado;** **volado** *[deh-spee-tah-doh; vo-lah-doh]*	**Traumtänzer** *[trowm-ten-tsah]*
Spastic *[spah-sstihk]* Someone clumsey and uncoordinated.	**Bobalicón** *[bo-bah-lee-kohn]*	**Tapsig** *[top-tseeg]*
Speed freak *[speed freek]* An amphetamine addict.	**Drogata;** **pepero** *[dro-ga-tah; peh- peh-ro]*	**Speed Freak** *[speed freek]*
Spic *[spihk]* Derogatory for someone of Spanish or Puerto Rican extraction	**Hispano** *[i-spah-no]*	**Spania** *[shpah-niah]*
Split beaver *[spliht-bee-vehr]* A pornographic photograph of a woman with her legs spread wide open..	**Piernas abiertas** *[pee-er-nas ah-bee- er-tas]*	**Gespaltener Biber** *[gesh-pahl-teh-nah bee-bah]*

French	Dutch	Japanese
Fils de pute! *[feesd pooht]*	**Hoerejong** *[hoo-eh-reh-ee-ong]*	こん畜生 *[kohn-chee-koo-shoh]*
Dans les vapes *[dahnl vahp]*	**In de wolken** *[ihn deh wohl-kehn]*	ハイ *[high]*
Mongolo *[mohn-goh-loh]*	**Spast** *[ss-pahst]*	まぬけ *[mah-noo-keh]*
Camé au speed *[cah-meh oh ss-peed]*	**Pillejunk** *[peeh-leh-jehnk]*	ヤクカン *[yah-koo-kahn]*
Spengouin *[ss-pahn-goo-ahn]*	**Paellavreter** *[pah-ehl-ee-ah-vhreh-eet-ehr]*	スペイン *[soo-peh-een]*
Photo de cul *[phoh-tohd coohl]*	**Spleetdiertje** *[ss-pleh-eet-dee-ehrtje]*	エロ写真 *[eh-loh-jah-sheen]*

English	Spanish	German

Spud
[spuhd]
Potato.

Papa
[pah-pah]

Kartoffel
[kar-tow-fehl]

Stacked
[stahkt]
A woman with a good figure, particularly large breasts.

Hembrón
[em-brohn]

Viel Holz vor der Tür
[feel holts for der tiur]

Stash
[stahsh]
Private collection, usually drugs.

Droga
[droh-gah]

Privatsammlung
[pree-vaht-zahm-loong]

Steamed up
[steemd uhp]
Angry.

Enfurecido, -a
[en-fur-eh-see-doh, -dah]

Im Dampf
[eem dahmpf]

Stewed
[stood]
Inebriated.

Borracho
[bor-rah-cho]

Geschmort
[geh-shmort]

Stick up
[stihk uhp]
A robbery.

Asalto
[ah-sal-toh]

Klebige Finger
[kleh-bee-geh feen-gah]

Stinker
[steen-kehr]
An unpleasant person.

Indeseable
[in-de-say-ah-blay]

Stinker
[steen-kah]

Stoned
[stohnd]
High on drugs.

Dopado; colocado, ciego
[do-pah-doh; koh-loh kah- doh, see-eh-go]

Auf dem Trip
[owf dem treep]

French	Dutch	Japanese
Patate *[pah-taht]*	**Aardappel** *[aahrd-appel]*	ジャガイモ *[jah-gah-ee-moh]*
Bien monté *[bee-ahn mohn-teh]*	**Stoot** *[ss-toh-oot]*	でかパイ *[deh-kah-pai]*
Cachette *[cah-sheht]*	**Voorraadje** *[voohr-raad-ee-eh]*	自分の麻薬 *[jee-boo-no-yah-koo]*
En colère *[ahn coh-lehr]*	**Laaiend** *[laah-ee-ehnd]*	爆発する *[bah-koo-hah-tsoo-soo-roo]*
Rétamé *[reh-tahm-eh]*	**Straalbezopen** *[ss-trahl-behzoh-oo-pehn]*	できあがった *[deh-kee-ah-gah-tah]*
Cambriolage *[cahm-bree-oh-lash]*	**Je geld of je leven** *[ee-eh chkehld ohf ee-eh leh-ee-vehn]*	強盗 *[go-toh]*
Salaud *[sah-loh]*	**Ruft** *[hruhft]*	ヘコキ *[heh-ko-kee]*
Stoned *[ss-tohn]*	**Stoned** *[ss-toh-oond]*	ヤクに酔う *[yah-koo-nee-yo-oo]*

English	Spanish	German

Stooge
[stooj]
A fool. The butt of a joke.

Idiota
[ee-dee-o-tah]

Narr
[nahr]

Stool pigeon
[stool pih-jihn]
A police informer.

Soplón
[so-plon]

Anscheißer
[ahn-shai-sah]

Straight
[strayt]
Heterosexual.
Uptight and conventional.

Macho
[mah-cho]

Hetera
[cheh-teh-rah]

Strap-hanger
[strahp-hahn-gehr]
Someone who rides the subway.

Peaton
[peh-ah-tohn]

Gurthänger
[goord-chen-gah]

Stud
[stuhd]
A man who thinks he is sexually well endowed and irresistable to women.

Tio cañon
[tee-oh kah-nyon]

Hengst
[hengst]

Suck
[suhk]
Perform fellatio.

Mamar
[mah-mar]

Lutschen
[loot-shen]

Sucker
[suh-kehr]
A gullable person.

Mamón
[mah-mohn]

Blutsauger
[bloot-zow-gah]

French	Dutch	Japanese
Nigaud *[neeh-goh]*	**Sufkop** *[soohf-kohp]*	アホ *[ah-ho]*
Mouchard *[mooh-shahr]*	**Tipgever** *[teep-chkeh-ee-vehr]*	密告者 *[mee-ko-koo-shah]*
Hétéro, honnête *[eh-teh-roh, oh-neht]*	**Hetero** *[heh-eet-hroh]*	ストレート *[stoh-leh-toh]*
Metro-boulot- dodo *[meh-throh-boo-loh-doh-doh]*	**Forensje** *[foo-hrehn-see-eh]*	乗車客 *[joh-shah-kyah-koo]*
Mec macho *[mek mah-shoh]*	**Stier** *[ss-tee-ehr]*	精力魔 *[say-ryo-koo-mah]*
Sucer *[soo-sehr]*	**Pijpen** *[pah-ee-pehn]*	吸う *[soo-oo]*
Salaud *[sah-loh]*	**Eikel** *[ah-ee-kehl]*	つり上げ屋 *[soo-ree-ah-geh-yah]*

English	Spanish	German
Sugar daddy *[shuh-gahr dah-dee]* An older man who supports a young man or woman in return for sexual favors.	**Papacito** *[pah-pah-cee-toh]*	**Alter Schwerenöter** *[al-tah shver-ren-oo-tah]*
Suit *[soot]* Someone who dresses conservatively and works a nine-to-five job	**Ejecutivillo** *[eh-heh-koo-tee-vee-yo]*	**Anzugträger** *[ahn-tsook-treh-gah]*
SWAK *[swahk]* Abbreviation for "sealed with a kiss".	**Morro** *[mor-ro]]*	**Mit einem Kuß besiegelt** *[meet ai-nem koos beh-zee-gelt]*
Switch hitter *[swihch hih-tehr]* A bisexual.	**Doble corriente, bisexual** *[do-blay kor-ree-en-tay, bee-sex-oo-all]*	**Wechselschalter** *[vek-sell-shahl-tah]*

French	Dutch	Japanese
Papa-gâteau *[pah-pah gah-toh]*	**Suikeroom** *[sah-eek-ee-ehr-oohm]*	パパ *[pah-pah]*
Cul de plomb *[coold plohm]*	**Kantoorpikkie** *[kahn-tohr-peek-kee]*	セビロ *[seh-bee-loh]*
Cellé d'un baiser (CDB) *[seh-leh dahn beh-seh]*	**Verzegeld met liefde** *[vehr-zeh-ee-chkehl meht leef-deh]*	キスマーク *[kee-soo-maah-koo]*
Quelqu'un qui marche à voile et à vapeur *[kehl-k-ahn kih mahrsh ah voo-ahl eh ah vah-pehr]*	**Bi** *[bee]*	バイ *[bai]*

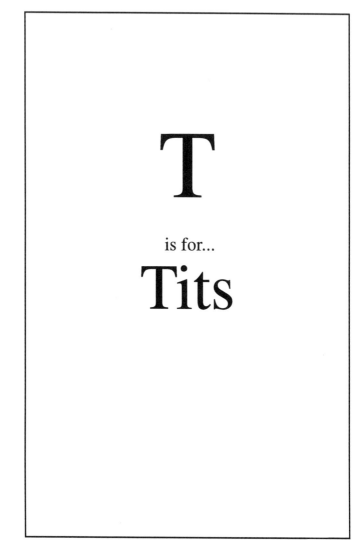

T

is for...

Tits

231

English	Spanish	German
Tail *[tayl]* Buttocks. Follow someone.	**Ojete** *[o-heh-tay]*	**Gesäß** *[geh-zahs]*
Take *[tayk]* Monetary profits, often from something illegal.	**Tajada** *[tah-hah-dah]*	**Beute** *[boy-teh]*
Tanked up *[taynkt uhp]* Drunk.	**Mocazo** *[moh-kah-zoh]*	**Voll betankt** *[fohl beh-tankt]*
Tart *[tahrt]* A prostitute.	**Ramera** *[rah-meh-rah]*	**Torte** *[tour-teh]*
Thick *[thihk]* Stupid.	**Estúpido** *[ehs-too-pee-doh]*	**Ein Brett vorm Kopf haben** *[ain brett foam kopf chah-ben]*
Ticked-off *[tihkt-ohff]* Angered or offended.	**Molesto, -a** *[mo-lesh-toh, -stah]*	**Kannste abhaken** *[kahn-steh ab-chah-ken]*
Tight *[tyt]* Slightly inebriated.	**Ligeramente borracho** *[lee-heh-ra-men-teh bor-rah-cho]*	**Blau** *[blau]*

French	Dutch	Japanese
Fesses *[fehz]* **- suivre** *[soo-ihvr]*	**Aan zijn kont plakken** *[ahn zah-een kont plahk-kehn]*	尻 *[shee-ree]*
Toucher des pots-de-vin *[too-shehrd pot-vahn]*	**Poet** *[poot]*	賄賂 *[wah-ee-loh]*
Chargé *[shahr-sheh]*	**Bezopen** *[beh-zoh-oo-pen]*	酔っ払った *[yo-pah-rah-tah]*
Cocotte *[coh-coht]*	**Hoerekoppie** *[hoo-ehhr-eh-koh-pee]*	売女 *[bai-tah]*
Crétin *[creh-tahn]*	**Oliedom** *[oh-oo-lee-dohm]*	あほう *[ah-hoh]*
En rogne *[ahn rognh]*	**Op z'n pik getrapt** *[ohp zehn pehk geht-trahpt]*	ガミガミ言う *[gah-mee-gah-mee-yoo]*
Saoûl *[sah-oohl]*	**Aangeschoten** *[ahn-chkehs-hoh-oo-tehn]*	ほろ酔い *[ho-lo-yo-ee]*

English	Spanish	German

Tight ass
[tyt ahss]
A rigidly correct person.

Estrecho, -a
[es-treh-cho]

Üeberkorekte Person
[ee-bah-koh-rek-teh per-zohn]

Tinkle
[teen-kuhl]
Urinate.

Mear
[meh-ar]

Pissen
[pee-sehn]

Tits
[tihtz]
Breasts.

Tetas
[teh-tahs]

Titten
[tee-ten]

Touchus
[tuh-kihss]
Buttocks. (Yiddish)

Culo
[koo—loh]

Hinterteil
[heen-tah-tile]

Toke
[tohk]
To take a puff of a marijuana cigarette.

Una calada de porro
[oo-nah kah-lah-dah de poh-ro]

Puf
[poof]

Tom cat
[tahm kaht]
When a man goes looking for sex.

Ligón
[lee-gohn]

Den Kater spielen
[den kah-tah spee-len]

Tool
[tool]
Penis.

La herramienta
[la eh-rrah-mee-en-tah]

Gerät
[geh-ret]

Trash
[trahsh]
To make a mess or destroy.

Cagarla
[kah-gar-lah]

Zerslörung
[tser-shlur-roong]

French	Dutch	Japanese
Grippe-sou [grihp-peh-sooh]	**Stijve lul** [ss-tah-ee-veh loohl]	堅い奴 [kah-tah-ee-yah-tsoo]
Pisser [pih-seh[	**Piesen** [pees-sehn]	つつはらい [tsoo-tsoo-hah-lah-ee]
Tetons [teh-tohn]	**Prammen** [phrah-mehn]	おっぱい [oh-pai]
voir "TAIL"	**Toges** [toh-oo-chkehs]	尻 [shee-ree]
Taffe [tahf]	**Een heis** [ehn hah-ees]	一服 [ee-poo-koo]
Un matou [ahn mah-too]	**Geile beer** [chah-eh-ee-leh beh-ehr]	盛りの付いた男 [mo-ree-no-tsoo-ee-tah-oh-toh-koh]
Outil [oot-ih]	**Gereedschap** [chkeh-hreh-eeds-chkahp]	男根 [dahn-kohn]
Foutre le bordel [foohtr leh bohr-dehl]	**Mollen** [mohl-lehn]	めちゃめちゃにする [meh-chah-meh-chah -nee-soo-roo]

English	Spanish	German
Trick *[trihk]* A prostitute's customer.	**Polvo, casquete** *[pohl-vo, kas-ket-teh]*	**Freier** *[frai-yah]*
Trip *[trihp]* A hallucinogenic experience.	**Viaje** *[vee-ah-heh]*	**Drogenreise** *[droh-gen-rai-zeh]*
Turd *[tuhrd]* Literally feces. An expression of contempt.	**Cagarro** *[kah-gah-rro]*	**Geistiger Dünnschiß** *[guy-shtee-gah din-shees]*
Twat *[twaht]* Female genitalia.	**Chocho, concha** *[cho-cho, kon-chah]*	**Möse** *[moo-zeh]*
Twit *[twiht]* Stupid person.	**Capuyo** *[kah-poo-yo]*	**Hauswurst** *[hows-voorst]*
Two-bit *[too biht]* Cheap or common.	**Mierdecilla -o** *[mee-ehr-deh-see-yah]]*	**Billig** *[bee-lish]*

French	Dutch	Japanese
Un truc *[ahn trihk]*	**Hoereloper** *[whooh-reh-loh-pehr]*	ヒモ *[hee-moh]*
Tripper *[trih-peh]*	**Trip** *[t-hrihp]*	ヒカリ *[hee-kah-ree]*
Merde, fumier *[mehrd, foo-mee-ehr]*	**Schijtluis** *[ss-chkah-eet-lah-oos]*	くそったれ *[koo-so-tah-reh]*
Moule *[moohl]*	**Trut** *[throoht]*	ハコ *[hah-koh]*
Andouille *[ahn-doo-ih-e]*	**Ei** *[ah-ee]*	あほ *[ah-ho]*
De quatre sous *[deh cat-r sooh]*	**Goedkoop** *[chkoot-kohp]*	安もん *[yah-soo-mohn]*

U

is for...

Upchuck

239

English	Spanish	German
Uncle *[uhn-kuhl]* To give in and admit defeat (cry uncle).	**Me rindo** *[meh reen-doh]*	**Seinen großen Bruder holen** *[zai-nen grow-sen broo-dah choh-len]*
Uncle Tom *[uhn-kuhl tahm]* Derogatory for black person who kowtows to white people	**Negro lameculos** *[neh-gro lah-meh-koo-los]*	**Devoter Schwarzer** *[deh-voh-tah shvar-tsah]*
Unreal *[uhn-reel]* Unbelievable.	**La leche, la hostia en bicicleta** *[la leh-cheh, la ost-ee-ah en bee-cee-kleh-tah]*	**Unwirklich** *[oon-vear-kleesh]*
Up yours *[uhp yohrz]* Expression of contempt.	**Que te den por culo** *[keh-teh then porr kooh-low]*	**Du kannst mich mal...** *[doo kanst meesh mahl]*
Uppers *[uhp-pehrs]* Amphetamines.	**Anfetas** *[ahn-feh-tas]*	**Hochbringer** *[choch-breen-gah]*
Upchuck *[uhp-chuhk]* Vomit..	**Echar la raba** *[eh-char la rah-bah]*	**Erbrochenes** *[ehr-broh-cheh-nes]*
Uptight *[uhp-tyt]* Someone who is rigid or fearful.	**Rígido** *[ree-hee-doh]*	**Nervös** *[ner-vooz]*

French	Dutch	Japanese
Crier pouce *[kree-ehr poos]*	**Handdoek in ring gooien** *[hahnd-dook ihn hring chkoh-ee-ee-ehn]*	お手上げ *[oh-teh-ah-geh]*
Oncle Tom *[ohncl Tohm]*	**Oom Tom** *[ohm tohm]*	白人にへつらう黒人 *[hah-koo-jeen-nee-h e h -tsoo-rah-oo-koh-koo-jeen]*
Dingue *[dahng]*	**Sodemieter op!** *[soh-deh-mee-tehr ohp]*	アンリアル *[ahn-lee-ah-loo]*
Va te faire enculer *[vaht fehr ahn-cool-ehr]*	**Lik m'n reet** *[lihk mehn reh-eet]*	どっか行け *[doh-kah-ee-keh]*
Amphets *[ahm-pheht]*	**Uppers** *[ah-pehrss]*	らりってる奴 *[lah-lee-teh-roo-yah-tsoo]*
Dégueuler *[deh-geh-lehr]*	**Kots** *[kohts]*	ゲロ *[geh-loh]*
Coincé *[cuahn-seh]*	**Angsthaas** *[ahngst-haahs]*	鬼 *[oh-nee]*

English	Spanish	German

User
[yoo-zehr]
Someone who takes
advantage of
others.

Un listillo
[oon lees-tee-yo]

Ausnutzer
[ows-noots-tsah]

French	Dutch	Japanese

Exploiter
[x-ploo-ah-tehr]

Mitnasjer
[meht-nah-sheehr]

こき使う奴
[koh-kee-tsoo-kah-oo-yah-tsoo]

V

is for...

Valley Girl

English	Spanish	German

Valley girl
[vah-lee guhrl]
Derogatory for young girl usually materialistic, superficial and with a distinctive style of speech. Popularized in song by Moon Unit Zappa.

Petarda, petorda
[peh-tar-dah, peh-tor-rah]

Blondie
[blon-dee]

Vamoose
[vah-mooss]
Go away, scram.

Vete a mamarla
[beh-teh a mah-mar-lah]

Hau ab
[how ub]

Veg out
[vej owht]
Space out. To sit like a vegetable.

Flipado
[flip-ah-doh]

Abheben
[ub-heh-ben]

Vibes
[vybz]
Atmosphere or mood.

Buen rollito
[bwen ro-yee-toh]

Vibrations
[vee-brah-tsee-yohns]

French	Dutch	Japanese
Pétasse *[peh-tahs]*	**Dom blondje** *[dohm blohndje]*	マテリアルガ ル *[mah-teh-ree-ah-loo-gah-loo]*
Casse-toi! *[cahs too-ah]*	**'M smeren** *[ehm ss-meh-rehn]*	バイバイ *[bai-bai]*
Glander *[glahd-eh]*	**Helemaal weg** *[heh-ee-leh-mahl vechk]*	ぼ-っとした *[boh-toh-shee-tah]*
Atmosphère *[at-mohs-fehr]*	**Bui** *[bah-oo]*	ム-ド *[moo-doh]*

W

is for...
Wimp

English	Spanish	German
Wack off [wahk ohff] Masturbate.	**Machacarsela** [mah-chah-kar-seh-lah]	**Onanieren** [oh-nah-nee-ren]
Wacko [wahk-oh] Crazy person.	**Majareta** [mah-hah-reh-tah]	**Deckel** [deh-kehl]
Wacky [wah-kee] Crazy.	**Descojone** [des-co-ho-nes	**Abgefahren** [ab-geh-fahr-ren]
Wagon [wah-gohn] Someone who is trying to remain sober, i.e., on the wagon.	**El mono** [el mo-no]	**In blanco** [ihn blan-koh]
Walk [wahlk] Someone who is not convicted of a crime (he walked).	**Se libro** [seh lee-bro]	**Zu Fuß** [tsoo foos]
Walk-up [wahlk ahp] An apartment without an elevator.	**Edeficio sin ascensor** [eh-deh-fee-see-oh seen ah-sen-sor]	**Treppe** [trep-peh]
Whallop [wah-lahp] Hit, or threaten to hit someone (Iíll give you a whallop).	**Hostion** [oh-stee-ohn]	**Faust** [fowst]

French	Dutch	Japanese
Se branler *[seh brahn-leh]*	**Afrukken** *[ahf-hrook-kehn]*	しごく *[shee-go-koo]*
Fêlé *[feh-leh]*	**Een gek** *[ehn chkehk]*	クルクルパ- *[koo-roo-koo-roo-pah]*
Farfelu *[fahr-feh-looh]*	**Gestoord** *[chkehs-stohrd]*	気違い *[kee-chee-gai]*
Grenouiller *[greh-noo-e-ieh]*	**Blauwe knoop** *[blah-oo-eh kno-ohp]*	禁酒 *[keen-shoo]*
être libéré *[ehtr lee-beh-reh]*	**Vrijuit gaan** *[vrah-ee-ah-oot chkahn]*	放免 *[hoh-men]*
Sans ascenseur *[sahns-ass-sahn-sehr]*	**Trappenhuis** *[threh-peh-haah-oos]*	ウオ- クアップ *[woh-koo-ah-poo]*
Une baffe *[oon-eh bahf]*	**Hoeke** *[hooh-keh]*	パンχ *[pahn-chee]*

English	Spanish	German
Washed up *[wahshd uhp]* Finished. (youíre all washed up)	**Estar acabado, -a** *[eh-star ah-kah-bah-doh]*	**Schwamm drüber** *[shvahm dree-bah]*
Waste *[waysst]* Kill someone.	**Liquidar a alguien** *[lee-kee-dar a al-gee-ehn]*	**Abfall** *[ab-fahl]*
Wasted *[way-stehd]* Drunk or high on drugs.	**Estar morado** *[eh-stah mor-rah-doh]*	**Besoffen** *[beh-zoh-fehn]*
Weed *[weed]* Marijuana.	**María** *[mah-ree-ah]*	**Unkraut** *[oon-krowt]*
Weirdo *[weer-doh]* Strange person.	**Raro, -a** *[rah-ro, -ra]*	**Verrückter** *[fehr-reek-tah]*
Well hung *[wehl huhng]* A well endowed male.	**Semental** *[seh-men-tahl]*	**Gutabgehangen** *[goot-ab-geh-hahn-gen]*
Wet back *[weht bahk]* Illegal immigrant, usually Mexican who illegally crosses the U.S.border.	**Espalda mojada** *[eh-spal-dah mo-hah-dah]*	**Illegaler Einwanderer** *[ee-leh-gah-lah ain-vohn-deh-rah]*

French	Dutch	Japanese
Bazaardé *[bah-tsar-deh]*	**Afgepeigerd** *[ahf-chkeh-pah-ee-chkehrd]*	あかん *[ah-kahn]*
Effacer *[eh-fah-seh]*	**Iemand koud maken** *[ee-mahnd kah-ood mah-ken]*	バクる *[bah-koo-loo]*
Camé *[cah-meh]*	**Straalbezopen** *[ss-thrahl-beh-zoh-oo-pehn]*	酔った *[yo-tah]*
Chiendent *[shee-ahn-dahn]*	**Wiet** *[veeht]*	はっぱ *[hah-pah]*
Drôle de coco *[drhohld coh-coh]*	**Halve zool** *[hahl-veh zohl]*	変人 *[hen-jeen]*
Monté comme un taureau *[mohn-teh cohm ahn toh-roh]*	**Goedgeschapen** *[chkooht-chkehs-schkah-pehn]*	あそこがでかい男 *[ah-so-ko-gah-deh-kah-yee-oh-toh-ko]*
Wetback *[oo-eht-bahk]*	**Bonenvreter** *[boh-neh-vreh-ee-tehr]*	潜り *[mo-goo-ree]*

English	Spanish	German

Wang
[wayng]
Penis.

Zipote
[zee-po-teh]

Schwänzchen
[shvens-shen]

Whack
[wahk]
Kill someone.

Matar a alguien
[mah-tar a al-gee-en]

Kaltmachen
[kahlt-mah-chen]

Wham bam thank you ma'am
[wahm bahm thahnk yoo mahm]
Very quick sexual intercourse. (See three minute man)

Un quiqui
[oon kee-kee]

Quickg
[kweek]

What's up?
[wahtss uhp]
How are you doing?

¿Qué pasa?
[kay pah-sah]

Was ist?
[vas eest]

Wilding
[wyl-deen]
Rampage involving theft and/or assault by group of teenagers.

Violencia juvenil
[vee-o-len-see-ah hoo-ven-eel]

Verwüstung
[fehr-veen-shtoong]

Wicked
[wih-kihd]
Excellent, superlative.

Pelotero
[peh-lo-teh-ro]

Ausgezeichnet
[owz-geh-tsaish-net]

Willies
[wih-leez]
Feeling of foreboding or discomfort.

Mal rollo
[mal ro-yo]

Unbehagen
[oon-beh-hah-gen]

French	Dutch	Japanese
voir"DICK"	Pik [pehk]	ちんぼ [cheem-bo]
Supprimer [soop-rhim-ehr]	Iemand afraggen] [ee-mahnd ahf- hrah-chkehn]	やる [yah-roo]
Coup de queue rapide [koopd keh rah- peed]	Vluggertje [vloochk-ehr-tje]	ちょろセックス [cho-lo-seh-ksoo]
ça va? [sah vah]	Hoe is-ie? [whoo is-ee]	元気? [gehn-kee]
Dépouiller [deh-poo-e-ieh]	Tremmen [threh-mehn]	不良 [hoo-ryoh]
Excellent [x-cell-ahn]	Gaaf [chkahhf]	最高 [sai-koh]
Avoir les chocottes [ah-voo-ahr leh shoh-coht]	Aan je water voelen [ahn ee-eh vah-tehr vooh-lehn]	いやな予感 [ee-yah-nah-yo- kahn]

English	Spanish	German
Wimp *[wihmp]* A sniviling, weak, inneffective or contemptible person.	**Un mierda** *[bo-kah-zas]*	**Schwächling** *[shveh-shleeng]*
Windbag *[wihnd bahg]* Arrogant person who talks too much.	**Bocazas** *[bo-kah-zas]*	**Windbeutel** *[veend-boy-tell]*
Wiped out *[wypt owht]* Tired.	**Estar muerto** *[ehs-tar moo-ehr-to]*	**Todmüde** *[toht-mue-deh]*
Wired *[wy-ehrd]* Full of nervous energy.	**Atacado** *[ahta-kah-do]*	**Unter Strom stehen** *[oon-tah shtruhm shteh-yen]*
With it *[wihth iht]* Someone who knows whatís going on. Trendy.	**Listillo** *[lee-stee-lo]*	**Wellenreiter** *[vehl-len-rai-tah]*
Wonk *[wahnk]* A "techno-nerd." Derogatory for someone involved in highly technical, bureaucratic, or procedural matters.	**Tecnócrata** *[teh-khno-krah-tah]*	**Technik-Freak** *[tech-neek-freehk]*

French	Dutch	Japanese
Une lavette *[oon-eh lah-veht]*	**Zakkenwasser** *[zoh-kehn-vahs-sehr]*	ベソ *[beh-so]*
Un moulin à pasoles *[ahn moo-lahn ah pah-sohl]*	**Windbuil** *[veehnd-beh-ehl]*	おしゃべり *[oh-shah-beh-ree]*
Crevé *[creh-veh]*	**Hondsmoe** *[hohnds-mooh]*	クタクタ *[koo-tah-koo-tah]*
à join *[ah shoo-ahn]*	**Opgefokt** *[ohp-chkeh-fohkt]*	針金 *[hah-ree-gah-neh]*
Branché *[brahn-sheh]*	**Trendy** *[threhnd-ee]*	トレンデイ- な奴 *[toh-len-dee-nah-yah-tsoo]*
Un gratte-papier *[ahn graht-pah-pee-eh]*	**Kantoorpikkie** *[kahn-toohr-pihk-kee]*	イシ頭 *[ee-shee-ah-tah-mah]*

English	Spanish	German
Working girl *[wohr-keen guhrl]* Prostitute.	**Puta** *[poo-ta]*	**Pferdchen** *[fert-shen]*
Wrecked *[rehkt]* Tired, hungover. Aftermath of binge involving drugs, alcohol or hard work..	**Guayavo, resaca** *[goo-ahya-voh]*	**Abgewrackt** *[ub-geh-vrackt]*
Wuss *[wuhss]* Abbreviation for ipussy.i Someone weak, cowardly or contemptible.	**Cobarde** *[koh-bahr-deh]*	**Schwächling** *[shvesh-leeng]*

French	Dutch	Japanese
Une racolleuse *[oon-eh rac-coh-iess]*	**Straathoer** *[ss-thraht-hoohr]*	売女 *[bai-tah]*
Défoncé *[deh-fohn-seh]*	**Verrot** *[veh-hrooht]*	二日酔い *[hoo-tsoo-kah-yo-ee]*
Un chiffre-molle *[ahn shifr-mohl]*	**Slappe lul** *[ss-lah-peh loohl]*	クズ *[koo-zoo]*

Y

is for...

Yellow
Belly

English	Spanish	German

Yack
[yahk]
Excessive talk or
gossip.

Chismear
[kee-zmeh-ahr]

Tratsch
[trotsh]

Yap
[yahp]
Mouth (shut your
yap).

¡Bocazas!
[hbo-kah-zas]

Schnauze
[shnow-tseh]

Yeech
[yeech]
Adjective to
describe something
extremely nasty or
unappealing.

¡Qué asco!
[qweh askoh]

Bääh
[beh-eh]

Yellow-belly
[yeh-loh-beh-lee]
Coward.

Cobarde
[koh-bahrd]

Feigling
[fai-gling]

Yenta
[yehn-tah]
A gossip.

Chisme
[kees-meh]

Klatsch
[klatsh]

Yo
[yoh]
Black slang used to
greet someone.

¡Hey!
[hehy]

Hallo
[hah-low]

Yuck
[yuhk]
Laughs. (Have a
few yucks).

Carcajada
[kahr-kah-hada]

Gelächter
[geh-lesh-tah]

French	Dutch	Japanese
Barratiner *[bah-hrah-tee-neh]*	**Grote bek** *[chkroh-teh behk]*	だべり *[dah-beh-ree]*
Ferme ta gueule *[fehrmt-ah-gehl]*	**Muil** *[meh-ool]*	口 *[koo-chee]*
Berk *[behrk]*	**Getver!** *[chkeht-fehr]*	うえ- *[oo-eh]*
Poule mouillé *[poohl moo-ee-ieh]*	**Lafaard** *[lah-fahrt]*	臆病者 *[oh-koo-byoh-mo-no]*
Une con-cierge *[oon-eh cohn-see-ehrgh]*	**Achterklap** *[ahchk-tehr-klahp]*	うわさ話 *[oo-vah-sah-bah-nah-shee]*
Eh *[eh]*	**Yoh!** *[ee-oh-oo]*	ヨウ *[yoh]*
Rigolades *[ree-gohl-ahd]*	**Ginnegappen** *[chkeen-eh-chkah-pehn]*	ハハハ *[hah-hah-hah]*

English	Spanish	German

Yuppie
[yuh-pee]
Abbreviation for young upwardly-mobile urban professional

Yupi
[yoo-pee]

Yuppie
[yoo-pee]

French	Dutch	Japanese
Yuppie *[yoop-ee]*	**Yuppie** *[ee-oo-pee]*	ヤッピ- *[yah-pee]*

Z

is for...

Zombie

267

English	Spanish	German
Zzzzz's *[zeez]* Sleep. Catch some Zzzzzís.	**Zzzzz's** *[zees]*	**Pennen** *[peh-nen]*
Zaftig *[zahf- tihg]* A Rubenesque woman.	**Gorda** *[gohr-dah]*	**Rubensfräuchen** *[roo-bens-froy-shen]*
Zapper *[zah-pehr]* Remote control for electronic appliance.	**El mando** *[ehl mahn-doh]*	**Zapper** *[tsah-pah]*
Zero *[zeh-roh]* Worthless person.	**Un cero a la izquierda** *[oon kehro a lah ee-cqwee-ehrdah]*	**Null** *[nool]*
Zilch *[zihlch]* Nothing.	**Nasty de plasty** *[nahs-stee deh plah-stee]*	**Nichts** *[neeks]*
Zip *[zihp]* Nothing.	**Nasty** *[nahs-tee]*	**Nix und wieder nix** *[neeks oond vee-dah neeks]*

French	Dutch	Japanese
Pioncer *[pee-ohn-seh]*	**Pitten** *[piht-tehn]*	グーグー *[goo-goo]*
Voluptueuse à la Rubens *[vol-oop-too-ehs ah lah roo-behns]*	**Mokkel** *[moh-kehl]*	ピχピχギャル *[pee-chee-pee-chee- gah-roo]*
Zappeur *[sahp-ehr]*	**Zapper** *[zoh-pehr]*	リモコン *[lee-mo-kohn]*
Un nul *[ahn nool]*	**Nul** *[noohl]*	ゼロ *[zeh-ro]*
Que dalle *[keh dahl]*	**Noppes** *[noh-pehs]*	クズ *[koo-zoo]*
Rien *[ree-ahn]*	**Nop-nul- noppes** *[nohp-nuhl-noh- pehsh]*	なし *[nah-shee]*

English	Spanish	German

Zipless fuck
[zihp-lehss fuhk]
A random sexual encounter.

Polvo imprevisto
[pohl-voh eehm-preh-vees-toh]

Schuß in den Offen
[shoos in den of-fen]

Zit
[ziht]
Pimple or acne.

Grano
[grah-noh]

Streuselkuchen
[shtroy-zehl-koo-chen]

Zombie
[zohm-bee]
Person who is oblivious or out of it.

Zombi
[zohm-bee]

Zombie
[tsom-bee]

Zonked
[zahnkt]
Drunk or stoned.

Colocado
[koh-loh-cah-doh]

Hackebreit
[hah-keh-bright]

French	Dutch	Japanese
Tirer un coup *[tee-reh ahn koop]*	**Palen laaien** *[pah-lehn lah-ee-ehn]*	あそこがユルイ *[ah-so-ko-gah-yoo-loo-ee]*
Un turbou *[ahn toor-boo]*	**Puist** *[pah-oost]*	にきび *[nee-kee-bee]*
Zombie *[sohm-bee]*	**Zombie** *[zohm-bee]*	ぼけ *[bo-keh]*
Pété *[peh-teh]*	**Stoned als een konijn** *[ss-tohnt ahls ehn koh-nah-een]*	酔った *[yo-tah]*

Be sure to look for these upcoming editions of **The Bad Words Dictionary**™:

1) **English, Polish, Hungarian, Czech, Russian, Hebrew.**

2) **English, Danish, Finish, Swedish, Gaelic, Arabic.**

3) **English, Portuguese, Greek, Italian, Turkish, Chinese .**

4) **English, Urdu, Aztec, Gypsy, Hindu, Sign Language.**

5) **English, Afrikaans, Latvian, Ukrainian, Thai, Korean .**

6) **English, Sizilian, Albanian, Corsican, Rumanian, Vietnamese.**